THE DISNEY BOOK OF KNITTING

THE Disney BOOK OF KNITTING

Melinda Coss and Debby Robinson

St. Martin's Press
New York

The Disney Book of Knitting

Copyright © 1987 by The Walt Disney Company

LIBRARY OF CONGRESS CATALOG CARD NUMBER:
87-42890

ISBN 0-312-01355-8

First U.S. Edition

Typeset by P&M Typesetting Ltd, Exeter, Devon

Printed in Italy by
New Interlitho

10 9 8 7 6 5 4 3 2 1

Produced by the Justin Knowles Publishing Group, 9 Colleton
Crescent, Exeter EX4 2BY, UK.

Contents

WALT DISNEY COPYRIGHT

The characters incorporated in the garments included in this book are copyright The Walt Disney Company, and the colors indicated on the charts are those officially approved by the Company.

For reasons of time and the unavailability of suitable yarns, some of the finished garments illustrated on the pages that follow do not conform exactly to Disney preferred colors. However, to ensure that the characters you choose to knit are as authentic as possible, you should make every effort to match the colors of the yarns you use as closely as possible to the colors shown in the charts.

In addition, to give your garment the final, authentic touch, when you have completed it, you should stitch the symbol "© Disney" using backstitch (see page 12). The ideal place on garments that have a single character motif is at the bottom and to one side of the motif. On garments with an all-over design, stitch the copyright logo at the lower left-hand side of the front.

TECHNIQUES

READING THE CHARTS

Throughout the book full color charts illustrate the motifs to be incorporated into the garments; stitch symbols have been added where necessary. Each square on the charts represents one stitch across – i.e., horizontally – and one row up – i.e., vertically. The charts should be used in conjunction with the written instructions, which explain where and when to incorporate them. Always assume that you are working in stockinette stitch unless otherwise instructed.

If you are not experienced in the use of charts, remember that when you look at the flat page you are looking at a graphic representation of the right side of your knitting, that is, the smooth side of stockinette stitch. For this reason, wherever possible, the charts begin with a right side (RS) row so that you can see exactly what is going on as you knit. Knit rows are worked from right to left, purl rows from left to right.

If a design covers an entire garment or part of a garment such as a sleeve, the chart represents the whole knitting area, from selvedge to selvedge. When a chart is used for a motif that is worked on a one-color background, it is boxed and the written instructions tell you exactly where this box fits into the work. It is vital that you work every stitch indicated within the border of the box, whether it is in main color or contrast, to ensure that the motif is correctly positioned on the finished garment.

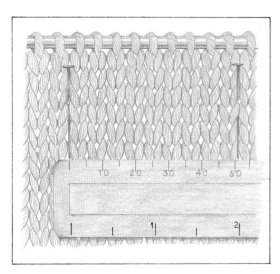

GAUGE

Knitting is simply the process of making a series of interconnecting loops, the formation of which is completely under the knitter's control. Gauge is the term used to describe the actual stitch size – its width regulating the stitch measurement, and its depth regulating the row measurement. Obtaining a particular gauge is not a magical skill, denied to all but the initiated. It is a technicality, the controlling factor of which is the size of needles used by the knitter.

Since all knitting instructions are drafted to size using mathematical calculations that relate to one gauge and one gauge only, you must achieve the stated gauge before you start work or you will have no control over the size of the finished garment. *This is the most important rule of knitting.*

At the beginning of every pattern a gauge measurement is given, using a specific stitch and needle size – e.g., "using No. 8 needles and measured over st st: 18 sts and 24 rows = 4in square." You must work a gauge sample using the same stitch and needle size as quoted. Cast on the appropriate number of stitches plus at least two extra, because edge stitches do not give an accurate measurement. When it is complete, lay the gauge sample or swatch on a flat surface and, taking great care not to squeeze or stretch it, measure the gauge, using a ruler and pins as shown.

If there are too few stitches, your gauge is too loose. Use needles that are one size smaller to work another swatch. If there are too many stitches, your gauge is too tight. Use needles that are one size larger to work another swatch.

Even if you have to change needle sizes several times, *keep working swatches until you get it right*. You save no time by skipping this stage of the work; if you do not get the correct gauge, you risk having to undo an entire garment that has worked out to the wrong size. You may feel that a slight difference is negligible, but a gauge measurement that is only a fraction of a stitch out in every inch will result in the garment being the wrong size, since each fraction will be multiplied by the number of inches across the work.

If you have to change your needle size to achieve the correct gauge for the main stitch, remember to adjust, in ratio, the needles used

Use a ruler and pins to measure the gauge of a sample piece of knitting.

for other parts of the garment that are worked on different sized needles. For example, if you are using one size smaller needles than are quoted for stockinette stitch, use one size smaller needles than are quoted for the ribbing.

Many people worry unnecessarily about row gauge, changing their needle size even though they have achieved the correct stitch gauge. Although important, row gauge does vary considerably from yarn to yarn and from knitter to knitter. If your stitch gauge is absolutely accurate, your row gauge will be only slightly out. Nevertheless, keep an eye on your work, especially when working something like a sleeve that has been calculated in rows rather than inches, and compare it with the measurement chart in case it is noticeably longer or shorter.

The fairisle method of color knitting can make a great deal of difference to your gauge. If you are working a motif in fairisle on a one-color background, take extra care with the gauge, working as loosely as possible so that the motif area does not pull more tightly than the stitches around it so causing your work to pucker and the actual motif to become distorted. To avoid this, it is advisable to use the intarsia method wherever practical (*see* page 9).

SHORT ROWS

Working short rows is also sometimes called "turning," since this is precisely what is done. By turning the work mid-row and leaving part of it unworked, your piece of knitting is shaped, because one side has more rows than the

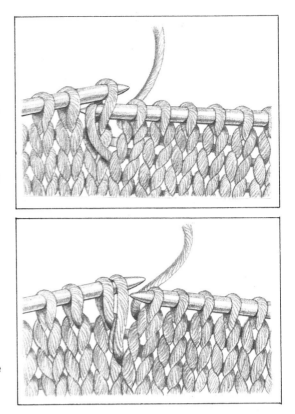

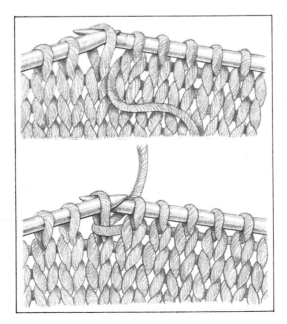

Right: to ensure that holes do not form at turning points, bring the yarn to the front of the work and slip the next stitch from the left-hand to the right-hand needle. Then put the yarn to the back of the work and return the slipped stitch to the left-hand needle before turning the work. Above right: add an extra row if you are working a turned shaping before binding off or knitting a seam.

other. If the work is then bound off, the edge will slope, and this is, therefore, an ideal way to shape shoulders. Working short rows is not advisable if you are working complicated stitches or color patterns, because the process of turning is likely to throw them off.

Unfortunately, holes tend to form at the turning points, even if care is taken. There is a way of overcoming this, and, although it appears complicated at first, it is well worth the effort of learning to master the technique. The method may be used on right or wrong side rows; here it is illustrated on the right side of stockinette stitch.

1. Knit to the point where turning is indicated, but before doing so bring the yarn to the front of the work and slip the next stitch from the left-hand to the right-hand needle.
2. Put the yarn to the back of the work and return the slipped stitch to the left-hand needle.
3. Now turn the work and purl to the end.

Repeat the last three steps at every turning point. All the stitches must now be worked across, and so if the short row shaping is worked immediately before binding off or knitting a seam, you should add an extra row. Work to the first stitch that has had a loop made

8

around it by putting the yarn forward and then back as above. Then:

1. Slip this stitch from the left-hand to the right-hand needle.
2. Using the point of the left-hand needle, lift the loop up onto the right-hand needle, making an extra stitch.
3. Replace the two stitches onto the left-hand needle, making sure that they are not twisted, and knit them together.

Work to the next "looped" stitch and repeat the process. When this row is completed, the work may be continued as usual.

INTARSIA

Intarsia is the term used to describe the technique of color knitting by which each separate area of color is worked using a separate ball of yarn. The colors are not carried from one area to another as with fairisle knitting. Any design that involves large blocks of isolated color that are not going to be repeated along a row or required again a few rows later should be worked in this way.

There is no limit to the number of colors that may be used on any one row, apart from that imposed by lack of patience or dexterity. Apart from the problem of getting into a tangle if there are too many separate balls of yarn hanging from the back of your work, you should also remember that every time a new ball of yarn is introduced and broken off after use, two extra ends are produced that will have to be secured when you are finishing the garment. When ends are left, always make sure that they are long enough so that they may be properly fastened off with a pointed tapestry needle. Do this carefully through the backs of the worked stitches so that the design on the right side of the work is not distorted. On no account should you knot the ends to secure them; in addition to looking unsightly, the knots will invariably work themselves loose.

If only a few large, regular areas of color are being worked, the different balls of yarn may be laid on a table in front of you while you work or kept separate in individual jam jars or even shoe boxes. This prevents the yarn getting into a tangle but requires careful turning at the end of every row so that the strands do not become twisted.

The easiest method is to use small bobbins that hold each color separately and hang at the back of the work. These may be bought from

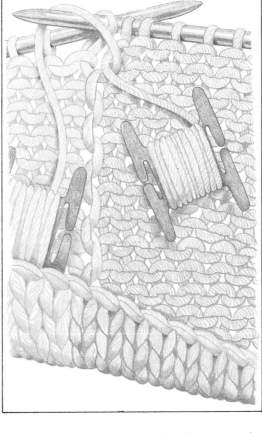

If you are using the intarsia method, twist the strands firmly together when you change colors.

most large yarn stores or made at home out of cardboard. They come in a variety of shapes, but all have a narrow slit in them to keep the wound yarn in place but allow the knitter to unwind a controlled amount as and when required. When winding yarn on a bobbin, try to wind sufficient to complete an entire area of color but don't overwind, as heavy bobbins will pull stitches out of shape.

When you change color from one stitch to another, it is vital that you twist the strands around each other before dropping the old color and working the first stitch in the new color. This prevents a hole forming. If you do not twist them there is no strand to connect the last stitch worked in color "A" to the first stitch worked in color "B." Twist the strands quite firmly to prevent a gap appearing after the work has settled.

FAIRISLE

The technique of color knitting called "fairisle" is often confused with the traditional style of color knitting that originated in the Fair Isles and took its name from those islands. Instructions that call for the fairisle method do not necessarily produce the multi-colored, geometric patterns that are associated with the Fair Isle style of knitting. The technique is suitable for any style of work in which small repetitive areas of color make the use of individual balls of yarn (intarsia method), impracticable.

Fairisle may be defined as knitting in which two colors are used across a row, the one not in use being carried at the back of the work until it is next required. This is normally done by dropping one color and picking up the other with your right hand. If you are lucky enough to have mastered both the "English" and "Continental" methods of knitting, both hands may be used so that neither yarn has to be dropped. One color is held in the left hand while the other color is held in the right hand at all times. The instructions below, however, cover the more standard one-handed method and give the three alternate ways of dealing with the yarn not in use.

Weaving the yarn creates a woven effect on the wrong side of your work.

Stranding

Stranding is the term used to describe the technique by which the yarn not in use is simply left hanging at the back of the work until it is next needed. The yarn in use is then dropped and the carried yarn taken up, ready for action. This means that the strand or "float" produced on the wrong side of the work pulls directly on the stitches either side of it.

It is essential that the float is long enough to

If you use the stranding technique, leave a loop on the wrong side of the work rather than pull the yarn too tightly.

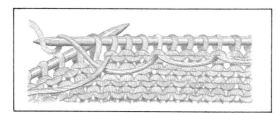

Be careful not to work too tightly with either the stranding or the weaving method.

span the gap without pulling stitches out of shape and to allow the stitches in front of it to stretch and prevent them from puckering on the right side of the work. It is preferable to go to the other extreme and to leave a small loop at the back of the work rather than pulling the float too tightly.

If the gap to be bridged by the float is wide, the strands produced may easily be caught and pulled when the garment is put on or taken off. This may be remedied by catching the floats down with a few stitches on the wrong side of the work when you are finishing the garment.

Weaving

With weaving the yarn being carried is looped over or under the working yarn on every stitch,

creating an up and down woven effect on the wrong side of the work. Since the knitter does not have to gauge the length of the floats, many people find that this is the easiest method of ensuring an even, accurate gauge. Weaving does increase the chances of the carried color showing through on the right side of the work, however, and it tends to produce a far denser fabric, which is not always desirable, especially if a thick, warm fiber such as mohair is being used.

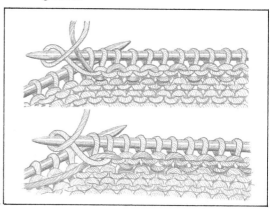

Stranding and weaving

Combining the two methods of stranding and weaving is invariably the most practical solution to the problem of working perfect fairisle. Most designs have color areas that contain varying numbers of stitches. If the gap between areas of the same color is only a few stitches, then stranding will suffice, but if the float produced will be too long, weave the carried yarn in every few stitches. Should you be unsure about the length of float to leave, slip your fingers under one: if you succeed with ease, the float is too long.

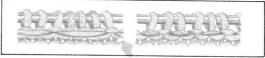

The most difficult aspect of fairisle knitting is to get the gauge correct. This does not depend on the stitch size so much as on the way you treat the carried yarn. This is why, when you work an all-over fairisle pattern, you should always knit a gauge sample in fairisle, not in main color stockinette stitch, because the weaving or stranding will greatly affect the finished measurement of the stitches.

The most important rule to remember is that *the yarn being carried must be woven or stranded loosely enough to have the same degree of "give" as the knitting itself.* Unless you achieve this, the resulting fabric will have no elasticity whatsoever, and very tight floats will buckle the stitches so that they lie badly on the right side of the work. On complicated designs, when more than two colors are used on a row, it may be necessary to carry more than one yarn at the back of the work. This should be avoided if at all possible, because ensuring that each color is woven in at the correct place is time consuming and results in an even heavier fabric. In such instances it may be advisable to combine the methods of intarsia and fairisle.

BUTTONHOLES

A badly worked buttonhole can spoil the look of a garment, pulling the buttonband out of shape and looking loopy. It is also of no practical use if it is worked too tightly or, as more often happens, too loosely so that the buttons are not held.

Because finding buttons that are perfectly suited to the garment you are working can prove difficult, it is advisable to find the buttons before you work the buttonholes. The buttonhole size may then be adjusted slightly to suit the buttons rather than the other way round. The adjustment is easily made by binding off one or two stitches more or less than stated in the instructions – provided, of course, that there are enough stitches across the buttonband to accommodate such an alteration.

All the buttonholes used in this book are of the most basic, horizontal variety, worked over two rows. On the first row the required number of stitches is bound-off off at intervals corresponding to the distance between each button. On the next row the same number of stitches is cast-on, immediately above those that were bound off on the previous row. If you use the thumb method of casting on, the first cast-on stitch often forms a loop unless it is worked with the yarn pulled very tightly on the needle. Alternatively, the work may be turned so that a two-needle method of casting on may be used to replace the bound-off stitches before turning the work back again and continuing the row as usual until the next buttonhole point is reached.

When you work a buttonhole across ribbing, which is the most common practice, keep in pattern throughout, although the binding off should be either knitwise or purlwise to give a firmer finish than a ribbed bound-off edge, which will be too elastic. Remember, all buttonholes should be a fraction too tight for their buttons when first completed, to allow for the inevitable stretching that occurs as a result of wear and tear.

MAKING A BOBBLE

Wherever the abbreviation MB appears in a pattern, it refers to a particular type of bobble, described below. If worked on a right side (RS) row the bobble will hang on the right side, if worked on a wrong side (WS) row, push the bobble through to the right side.

1. When the MB position on the row has been reached, make five stitches in the next stitch by knitting into its front, then its back, front, back and front again before slipping it off the left-hand needle.
2. Turn the work and knit these five stitches only.
3. Turn the work, p2 tog, p1, p2 tog.
4. Turn the work, sl 1, k2 tog, psso.

Place this stitch on the left-hand needle, turn the work and continue as usual, the single stitch having been restored to its original position on the row.

SEAMS

After achieving the correct gauge, the most important technique to master is the final sewing up of your knitting. This can make or break a garment, however carefully it may have been knitted, and is the reason the finishing instructions in every knitting pattern should be followed precisely, especially the type of seam to be used and the order in which the seams are to be worked.

Before starting any piece of work always leave an end of yarn that will be long enough to complete a substantial part of the eventual seam, if not the whole thing. When you have worked a couple of rows, wind the end up and pin it to the work to keep it out of the way. If necessary, also leave a sizeable end when the work has been completed so that you may use it for seaming rather than joining in a new end, which may well work loose, especially at stress points.

The secret of perfect-looking seams is uniformity and regularity of stitch. When you join two pieces that have been worked in the same stitch they should be joined row for row. All work should be pinned first to ensure that the fabric is evenly distributed. When joining work that has a design on both pieces, take great care to match the colors, changing the color you are using to sew the seam where necessary.

When you are using backstitch to join a seam and you are starting at the very edge of the work, close the edges with an overstitch before starting the row of backstitch. The finished seam should be even and perfectly straight, the two lower diagrams illustrating the front and back respectively of the completed seam.

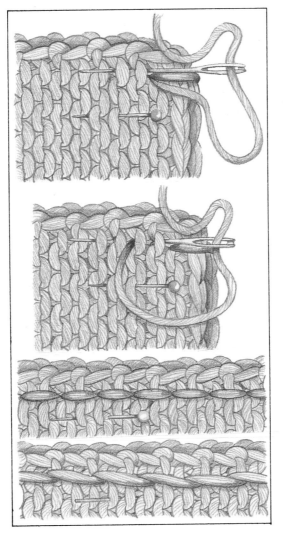

Backstitch

Pin the two pieces of work together, right sides facing, and make sure that the edges are absolutely flush. Always leave as narrow a seam allowance as possible to reduce unnecessary bulk. It is essential that the line of backstitches is kept straight and you should use the lines of the knitted stitches as a guide. All the stitches should be the same length, one starting immediately after the previous one has finished. The stitches should form a continuous straight line on the side of the work facing you. If the seam starts at the very edge of the work, close the edges with an overcast stitch, as shown, before working the backstitch:

1. Make a running stitch (maximum length ½in), through both thicknesses of work.
2. Put the needle back into the work in exactly the same spot as before and make another running stitch, twice as long as the first.

3. Put the needle back into the work at the same point at which the previous stitch ended. Make another stitch, the same length.

Keep repeating stage 3 until the last stitch, which should be half as long as the other stitches to fill in the gap left at the end of the seam.

By keeping the stitch line straight and by pulling the yarn fairly firmly after each stitch, no gaps should appear when the work is opened out and the seam pulled apart.

This seam is suitable for lightweight strands or where an untidy selvedge has been worked.

Flat seam

The expression "flat seam" is a slight contradiction in terms since it involves an oversewing action. However, when the work is opened out it will do so completely and lie quite flat, unlike a backstitched seam.

Use a blunt-ended tapestry needle to avoid splitting the knitted stitches. After pinning both pieces, right sides together, hold the work as shown. Pass the needle through the very edge stitch on the back piece and then through the very edge stitch on the front piece. Pull the yarn through and repeat the action, placing the needle through exactly the same part of each stitch every time. Always work through the edge stitch only. If you take in more than this, you will have a lumpy, untidy seam that will never lie flat.

When two pieces of stockinette are to be joined with a flat seam, do not work a special selvedge (such as knitting every edge stitch). Work the edge stitches as usual but as tightly as possible, using the very tip of your needle. When you come to work the seam, place the tapestry needle behind the knots of the edge stitches and not through the looser strands that run between the knots, for these will not provide a firm enough base for the seam, which will appear gappy when opened out.

Flat seams are essential for garments made of heavy-weight yarns on which a backstitch would create far too much bulk. They should also be used for attaching buttonbands, collars and so forth, when flatness and neatness are essential. Borders, waistbands, cuffs and any other part of the garment where the edge of the seam will be visible should also be joined with a flat seam, even if the remainder of the garment has backstitched seams. In these instances, start with a flat seam until the ribbing border is complete and then change over to

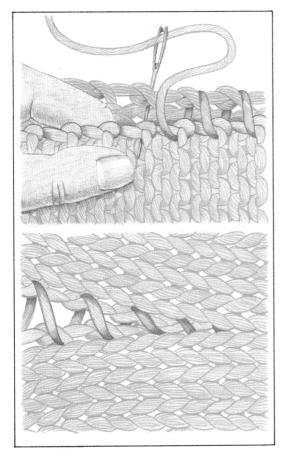

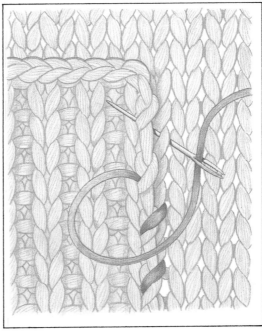

Far left: the diagrams show
how you should hold the
knitting to work a flat seam
and how your work will
look on the right side.

Left: use slip stitch to attach
a pocket to a garment.

backstitch, taking in a tiny seam allowance at first and then smoothly widening it, making sure that you do not suddenly increase the depth of the seam.

Sewn slip stitch

If one piece of work is to be placed on top of another – for example, when turning in a double neckband, folding over a hem or attaching the edges of pocket borders – you should use slip stitch.

When you are turning in a neckband that has been bound off, place the needle through the bound-off edge and then through the appropriate stitch on the row where it was initially picked up. It is essential that you follow the line of the stitch to avoid twisting the neckband. As you repeat the action, the visible sewn stitch runs at a diagonal.

The same rule applies when you sew down a neckband that has not been bound off but on which the stitches are held on a thread. The only difference is that the needle is placed through the actual held stitch to secure it. When each stitch has been slip-stitched down, the thread may be removed. This method results in a neckband with more "give" in it than one that has been bound off.

When you are slip-stitching a turned-in waistband, use the line of a row as a guide to produce a perfectly straight, horizontal line of stitches, which should not show through to the right side of the work. On pocket borders, use the line of stitches on the main piece as a guide to produce a perfectly straight vertical line of stitches. Pass the tapestry needle through one strand of the main piece stitch and then behind the knot of the border edge stitch, as for a flat seam.

KNITTED SHOULDER SEAMS

This method of joining is perfect for shoulders on which no shaping has been worked or on which the shaping has been made by working short rows (*see* page 8). It creates an extremely neat, flat seam.

Because the two pieces to be joined must be

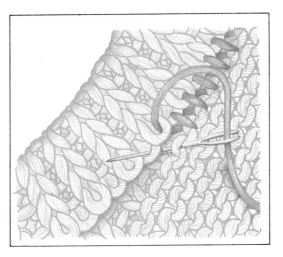

Use slip stitch to hold a
double neckband in
position.

The diagrams illustrate the three steps involved in knitting shoulder seams together. You must always have exactly the same number of stitches on the two pieces that are to be joined in this way.

worked stitch for stitch, they must both have exactly the same number of stitches. Even though the pattern will specify that you should have a certain number of stitches on your needles at this point, it is wise to double check the number you actually have, as it is very easy to lose or gain a stitch accidentally as you work.

The technique itself requires three needles. The stitches from the front and back are held on their respective needles, which should both be in your left hand, while in your right hand you should hold a third needle. This third needle should be larger than the others to help prevent the bound-off stitches being too tight. Holding more than one needle in the hand and trying to work through two stitches at a time without dropping them can seem very awkward at first, but, with a little practice, it will feel like regular knitting. Hold the needles so that the right sides of the work face one another and so that the stitches line up at corresponding intervals on the front and back needles. Work as follows:

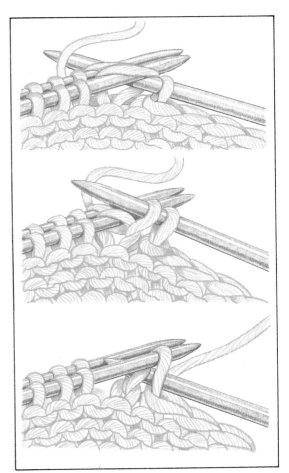

1. The point of the right-hand needle is put through the first stitch on the front needle and the first stitch on the back needle, with exactly the same action as a regular knit stitch but going through both simultaneously.
2. Pull a loop through to form a single stitch on the right-hand needle, slipping the old stitches off the left-hand needles.
3. Repeat steps 1 and 2 so that there are two stitches on the right-hand needle. The second stitch is then lifted over the first, as in regular binding off.

Step 3 should be repeated across all the stitches to be knitted together until one loop remains on the right-hand needle. Pull the yarn through this to secure it.

When you are knitting together a shoulder seam on a garment on which no neck shaping has been worked and on which the neck stitches have not been bound off, all the stitches on the back may be dealt with at the same time. Start to work the first shoulder together from the armhole to the neck edge, then bind off the back neck (if the pattern requires that they are bound off), without breaking the yarn, which may then be used to knit together the second shoulder seam from neck to armhole.

Although it is normally worked on the inside of the work to create an extremely neat, flat and durable seam, a knitted seam may also be

worked with the wrong sides of the knitting facing one another. This creates a decorative ridge on the right side of the work.

KNITTING UP STITCHES

The term "picking up" stitches is sometimes used instead of "knitting up" stitches, but it is rather a misleading phrase since it implies that the stitches are simply strands that have been pulled out around the edge of the work. This should never be done, for it produces uneven and untidy loops. The correct method is to use new yarn to create brand new stitches through the edge of the existing knitted fabric. This produces tidy, uniform stitches, and allows you to control the positioning of them.

As with working perfect flat seams, the preparation – i.e., the actual knitting – is the most important part of knitting up stitches. A firmly and neatly worked edge is essential for tidy knitting up. Always work edge stitches tightly, and if shaping has been worked – around a neckline, for instance – any decreases or increases should be worked one or two stitches in from the edge stitch wherever the pattern will allow. In this way the irregular, stretched stitches of the shaping are out of the way and the edge stitches worked in the usual manner can form the basis of the new stitches. Each new stitch should emerge from behind the knot of the edge stitch as this is the firmest part of the stitch. The strand between the knots will tend to stretch and should be used only when there is no alternative.

If you are working a color pattern on a main color, stop the pattern short a few stitches in from the edge so that the last few stitches are worked in main color only. Knitting up from stitches of various colors will create an untidy line. When you are completing a piece of work that is to have stitches knitted up at a later stage, leave the yarn attached so that it may be used when required and so that you do not have to join in a new end of yarn, which will have to be secured.

When a pattern states exactly how many stitches are to be knitted up, if you are to work them in a stitch for which you have not worked a separate gauge sample – e.g., ribbing when the pattern has required you to work a gauge sample in stockinette stitch – it is worthwhile to work a few knitted-up stitches as a test before beginning the knitting-up itself since ribbing gauge varies greatly compared with stockinette stitch.

If you find it difficult to distribute the number of stitches that are to be knitted up, divide your work into halves and then into quarters (and even eighths if it is a long edge), and mark these points with pins. Apportion the number of stitches equally among these sections. If they do not divide equally, use any extra stitches where they might be needed, such as at seam edges. Never distribute the stitches as you go along as this will invariably result in an uneven effect, with some areas bunched with too many stitches and others stretched with too few.

Once the edge has been prepared, hold the work with the right side towards you. Hold the yarn at the back of the work so that the stitches may be pulled through to the front. This may be done either with the needle you intend to use for the first row or, more easily, with a crochet hook. Use a crochet hook that will slip easily through the base stitch to catch the yarn and pull it through to the right side of the work where it is then slipped onto the needle holding the new stitches. Pull the yarn tight. The holding needle should be one or two sizes smaller than the size quoted for the actual knitting up to reduce the stitch size on the first row, thus creating a neater finish. Change to the correct needle size on your second row. The first row of a band or border that is to be

ribbed may also be either knitted or purled as this, too, creates a smaller stitch than an initial row of ribbing. Knitting this row with the right side facing you gives a smooth, inconspicuous row. If you purl this row, a ridge will be formed on the right side of the work, which will neaten the knitted-up edge in a more decorative way. Ribbing should then continue as normal.

If stitches are held between two areas of knitted-up stitches, as they may often be at the center front edge of a crew neck, slip these stitches onto another needle and then knit them onto the holding needle to save you from having to break the yarn; slip the held stitches onto the holding needle and join in the yarn again to knit up further stitches. It is also advisable to knit up a stitch from the loop at the beginning and the end of any set of stitches that have been bound off or are on a holder. These are stress points and often become stretched, and an extra stitch will prevent a hole forming.

If you are using a set of double-pointed needles to knit around some necklines, the same rules apply, but the stitches that are knitted up must be equally distributed among the number of needles in use, leaving one needle free for the working.

SHOULDER PADS

The type of knitted shoulder pad for which instructions are given in the pattern for the Seven Dwarfs Cardigan (page 78) may be adapted for use in any garment, provided you allow for different thicknesses of yarn by altering the number of stitches.

Once knitted, the straight edge of the pad should be turned back on itself to halve its depth and create a thicker edge. Slip stitch this into position.

The most important aspect of knitted shoulder pads is the way they are attached to the garment so that they sit correctly and do not pull the fabric out of shape. Do not turn the garment inside out. Fold the pad in half and slip it inside the garment, ensuring that the folded

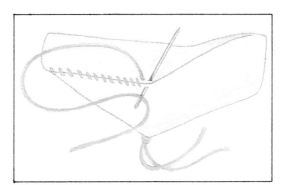

Turn the straight edge of a knitted shoulder pad back on itself and slip stitch it into position.

Pin a shoulder pad in
position before attaching it
at the shoulder and
armhole seams only.

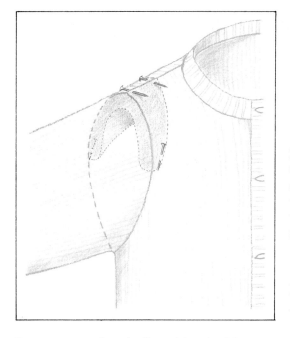

line corresponds to the line of the shoulder
seam and the thick edge lies along the line of
the armhole seam. Hold the garment up so that
it takes its own weight, as it will do when worn,
and pin the pad in position through the right
side of the garment. Only when it is firmly
positioned should the garment be turned
inside out and the pad tacked in place.

The point of the pad should be attached to
the shoulder seam and the two ends of the
thick edge should be sewn to the armhole
seam. Attach the pad at these three seam
points only. Never attach a pad to the knitted
fabric itself as this will pull the stitches out of
shape and be visible on the right side of the
work.

EMBROIDERY

To achieve the detail necessary for the facial
features of some of the characters incorporated
into the garments, simple embroidery stitches
have been added after the knitting has been
completed. You may find it helpful to sketch

onto the knitted fabric, using tailor's chalk or
lines of very small pins, the position and outline
of the embroidery.

Satin stitch

Satin stitch is used to fill in areas such as eyes.
It is formed by working straight stitches, very
close to one another, over the length of the
area to be covered.

Backstitch

Outlines are worked in backstitch, which
should be worked in exactly the same way as
the stitch used for seams (*see* page 12). When
you are working a curve, try to make very
small stitches to ensure a continuous line.

FRINGES

A row of fringing adds the classic finishing
touch to scarf ends and may be executed with
the help of a crochet hook.

Because many lengths of yarn must be cut to
a uniform length, find an object, such as a book,
which the yarn may be wrapped around over
and over again before cutting it along one side.
The lengths produced should be two-and-a-
half times longer than the required fringe
length, for the knotting takes extra yarn and it is
often necessary to trim the ends to produce a
really straight line of fringes. Decide how many
fringes you require and mark their positions on
the bound-off and cast-on edges of the scarf.

Take several strands of yarn, depending on
how fat you want the fringes, hold them flush
with each other and fold them in half. With the
right side of the work facing you, put the
crochet hook through the edge and pull the
fold point of the fringe through to form a loop on
the wrong side of the work. Now put the
crochet hook through the loop to pull the fringe
ends up and through it. Pull this knot firmly, but
not too tightly. When the whole row is complete,
trim to the desired length.

Right: when you embroider
the facial features of some
of the character motifs, use
satin stitch for solid areas
such as eyes and backstitch
for outlines.

Far right: the three stages
of knotting a fringe.

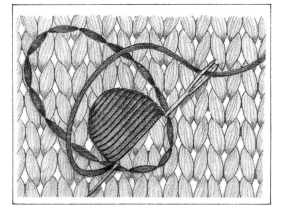

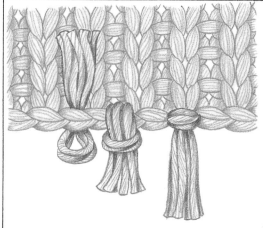

BIG BAD WOLF WOMEN'S SWEATER

An oversized, roll-neck raglan in a tweedy, aran-weight wool, with that bane of the Three Little Pigs, the Big Bad Wolf, looming menacingly on the front!

Materials
Yarnworks aran-weight wool – main color: 29oz; contrast colors: less than 1oz of each of the seven colors, matched exactly to the chart.

Needles
One pair of No.7 and one pair of No.9 needles; a set of double-pointed No.7 needles.

Gauge
Using No.9 needles and measured over st st: 16 sts and 24 rows = 4in square.
NOTE: To avoid puckering, keep your gauge the same when working the color motif. Do not carry the main color behind the motif.

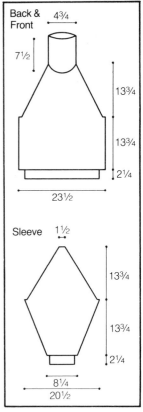

Back & Front

4¾

7½

13¾

13¾

2¼

23½

Sleeve 1½

13¾

13¾

2¼

8¼

20½

Back

Using main color and No. 7 needles, cast on 96 sts.

Row 1: *k2, p2, rep from * to end. Repeat this row to form double ribbing for 2¼in, ending on a WS row. Knit the next row, inc into every 16th st (102 sts). Now change to No. 9 needles and cont in st st until the work measures 16in, ending with a RS row.

Shape raglan: bind off 2 sts at beg of next 2 rows. Next row: purl. Row 2: k3, sl 1, k1, psso, k to last 5 sts, k2 tog, k3. Repeat the last 2 rows until 22 sts remain. Work 3 rows straight. Bind off.

Front

Same as for back until 6 rows of st st have been worked.

Next row (RS): k8, k the first row from the chart, k to end. Cont working chart in this position until it is complete (meanwhile working raglan shaping throughout), then cont in main color only. When raglan shaping has reduced to 34 sts **shape neck**: next row (WS) p12 sts, bind off 10 sts, p to end. Cont with this set of sts, leaving others on a holder. Dec 1 st at neck edge on the next 4 rows, meanwhile cont raglan shaping as before. Now work the neck edge straight and cont shaping raglan until 2 sts remain. Work 2 rows straight, P2 tog and pull yarn through remaining st to secure. Return to the other side of the neck, joining in yarn at neck edge. Work to match the first side.

Sleeves

Using main color and No. 7 needles, cast on 36 sts and work in double ribbing for 2¼in. Change to No. 9 needles and cont in st st, inc 1 st at each end of next and every following 3rd row until you have 90 sts. Work straight until the sleeve measures 16in, ending with a RS row. **Shape raglan**: as for back until 8 sts remain. Work 2 rows straight and then bind off.

Collar

Join all raglans with a flat seam. Using the set of double-pointed No. 7 needles and with the RS of work facing you, knit up 104 sts evenly around neckline. Knit the first row and then work in double ribbing until the collar measures 7½in. Bind off in ribbing.

Finishing

Join remaining seams with a flat seam throughout.

BAMBI TEENAGER'S SWEATER

Materials

Yarnworks mercerized worsted weight cotton – green 16/18oz; white: 6/6oz; pink 1/1oz; contrast colors: less than 1oz each of the six colors, matched exactly to the chart.

Needles

One pair of No.3 and one pair of No.5 needles.

Gauge

Using No.5 needles and measured over st st: 22 sts and 29 rows = 4in square.
NOTE: To avoid puckering, keep your gauge the same when working the color motif. Do not carry the main color behind the motif.

A delicate party sweater with a slightly scooped neck and raglan sleeves, in sizes petite/small throughout. Knitted in a worsted weight mercerized cotton in sugared almond colors, the sweater features Bambi in a shower of white bobbles.

Back

Using No.3 needles and white, cast on 88/98 sts. Row 1: * k1, p1, rep from * to end. Repeat this row to form single ribbing. Work 3 rows white in all, then 2 rows pink, 4 rows white, 2 rows pink. Change back to white and rib until work measures 2¼in, ending with a WS row.
Next row: change to green and knit, inc into every 14th/16th st (94/104 sts). Change to No.5 needles and cont in st st, working from the chart. Omit the Bambi motif but work all bobbles (i.e., those indicated by "X" as well as "O"), in white, as indicated on the chart (*see* Techniques page 11). Break off yarn after completing each bobble; do not carry the yarn at the back of the work. Because two sizes have been superimposed on the same chart, you should omit bobbles that fall very near to the edge of the size you are working. Cont working

from the chart throughout. When armholes are reached (work measuring approx 11½/12¼in), ending on a WS row, **shape raglan**: bind off 2 sts at beg of next 2 rows. Now dec 1 st each end of every 3rd row until 50/54 sts remain. Work 1 row straight. Bind off.

Front

Same as for back but work the Bambi motif and omit the bobbles represented by "X". Work chart throughout. Shape the raglan as for the back and when 62/66 sts remain **shape neck**: work 20/22 sts, bind off 22 sts, work to end. Cont with this set of sts, leaving the other sts on a holder. (Dec at raglan edge as before, throughout.) Dec 1 st at neck edge on every row until 12/7 sts remain. Now dec 1 st at neck edge on every alt row until 2 sts remain. Work straight for 1 row. Work 2 tog and secure by pulling yarn through the remaining st. Return to held sts, joining in yarn at neck edge and shaping to match.

Sleeves

Using No.3 needles and white, bound on 40/44 sts and work the ribbing exactly as for the back, ending on a WS row.
Next row: change to green and knit, inc into every 5th st (48/52 sts). Now change to No.5 needles and cont in st st, inc 1 st each end of every 6th row until you have 78/86 sts. Work straight until the sleeve measures 16/17in, ending with a WS row. Now start working the bobbles from the sleeve chart and simultaneously start to **shape raglan**: bind off 3/2 sts at beg of next 2 rows. Now dec 1 st each end of every other row until 12 sts remain. Work 3/1 rows straight. Bind off.

Neckband

Join raglan seams, excepting the right back sleeve, with a narrow backstitch. Using No.3 needles, white yarn and with RS of work facing, knit up 48/52 sts across the back neck, 10 sts over the sleeve top, 16 sts down the side of the neck, 22 sts across the front, 16 sts up the other side and 10 sts across the other sleeve top (122/126 sts). Purl the first row and then work in single ribbing for 2 rows. Change to pink and rib 2 rows. Return to white, rib 3 rows and bind off in ribbing.

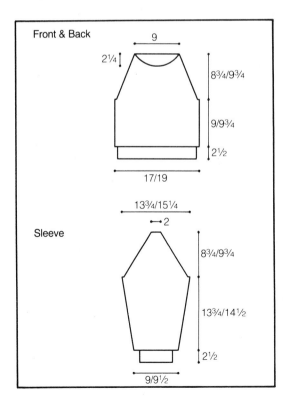

Front & Back

9

2¼

8¾/9¾

9/9¾

2½

17/19

Sleeve

13¾/15¼

2

8¾/9¾

13¾/14½

2½

9/9½

The symbols "X" and "0" on the charts on pages 21 and 23 indicate that bobbles should be worked at those points; *see* Making a bobble, page 11.

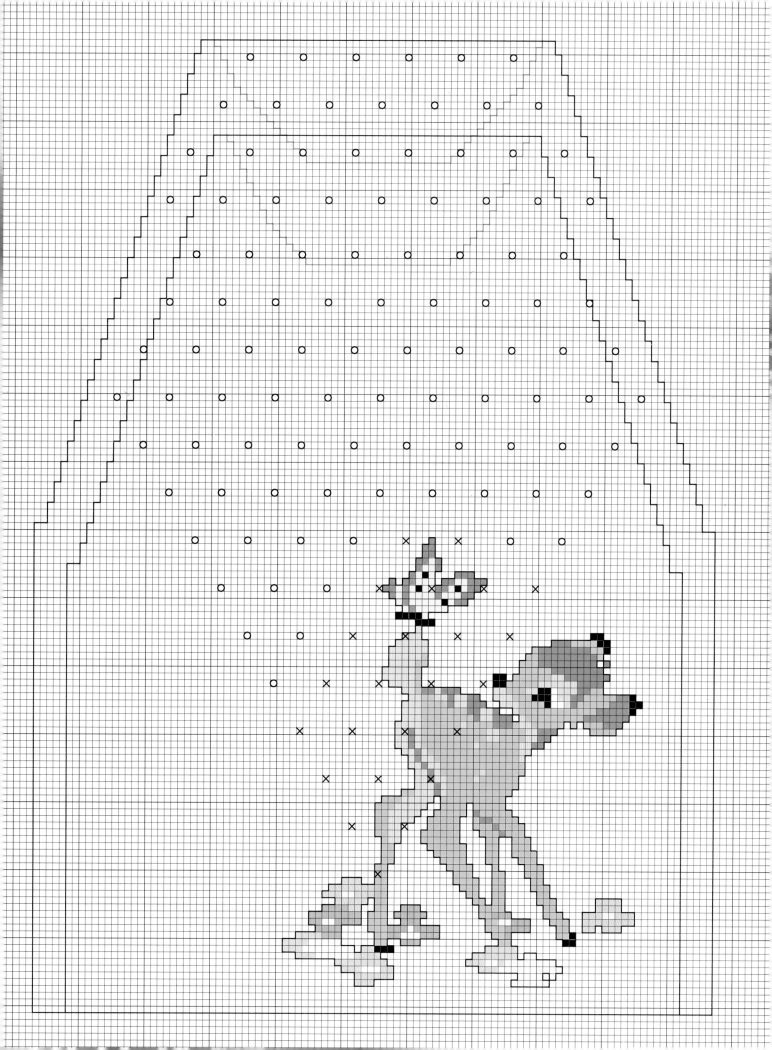

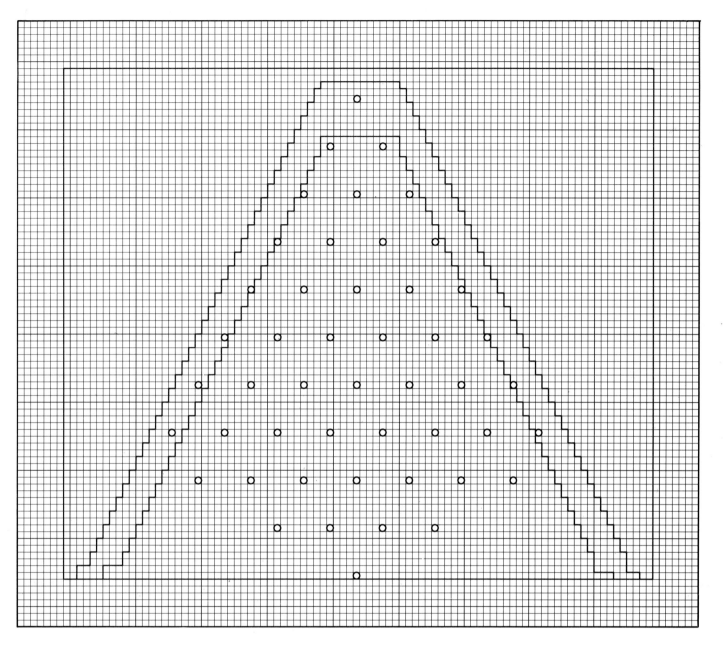

Finishing

Join all ribbed edges with a flat seam, using a narrow backstitch for the st st edges. Secure all bobble and motif ends taking great care not to pull any sts out of shape.

LADY AND THE TRAMP WOMEN'S SWEATER

A tunic-shaped, one-size sweater, in worsted weight wool. Worked in stockinette stitch, it has a seed stitch trim, including a neat little collar.

The hero and heroine of Walt Disney's classic are portrayed on the front.

Materials
Yarnworks worsted weight wool – turquoise: 22oz; contrast colors: less than 1oz of each of the 10 colors, matched exactly to the chart.

Needles
One pair No.6 and one pair No.4 needles.

Gauge
Using No.6 needles and measured over st st: 24 sts and 32 rows = 4in square.
NOTE: To avoid puckering, keep your gauge the same when working the color motif. Do not carry the main colors behind the motifs.

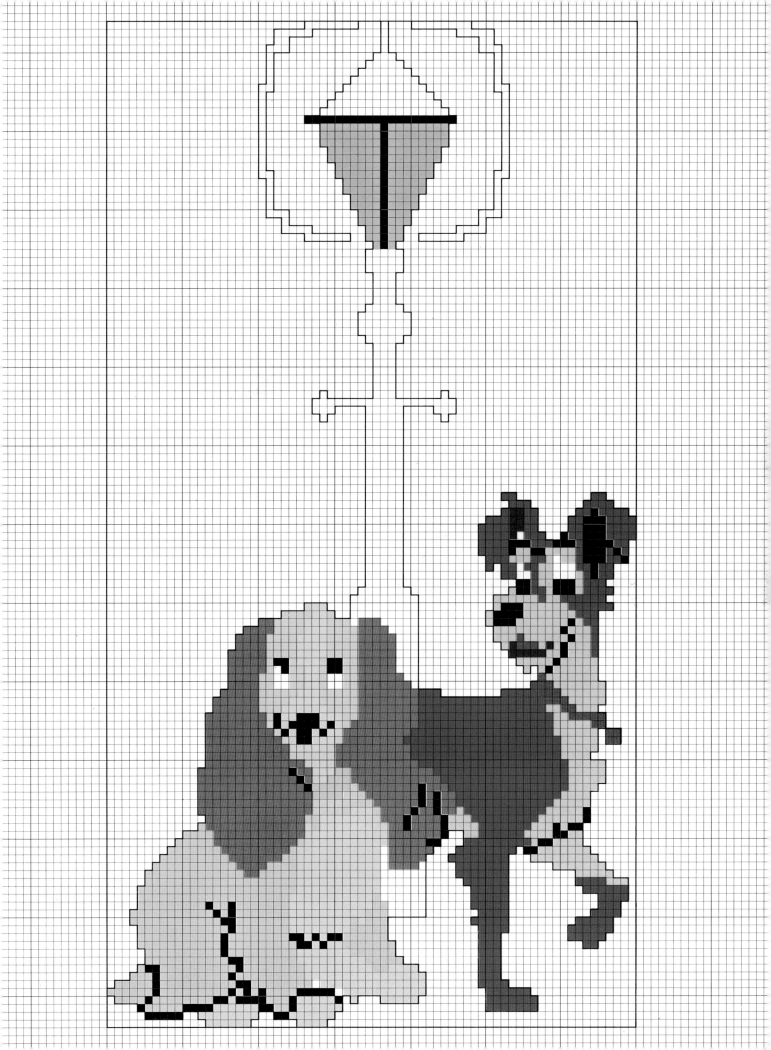

Back

Using No.4 needles and main color, cast on 148 sts.

Row 1: *k1, p1, rep from * to end. Row 2: *p1, k1, rep from * to end. Repeat these 2 rows to form seed st. When work measures 1¼in, change to No.6 needles and cont in st st until work measures 32in. Leave sts on a spare needle.

Front

Same as back until work measures 5in, ending with a WS row.

Next row: k39, k the first row of the chart, k to end. Cont working the chart in this position until it is complete. Now cont in main color until the work measures 27½in. **Shape neck**: work 64 sts, bind off 20 sts, work to end. Cont with this set of sts, leaving the others on a holder. Dec 1 st at neck edge on every other row until 54 sts remain. Work straight until this side is as long as the back. Leave sts on a holder. Return to the other side of the neck and shape to match. Leave sts on a holder.

Sleeves

Using No.4 needles and main color, cast on 50 sts.

Row 1: *k1, p1, rep from * to end. Repeat this row to form single ribbing for 1½in, ending on a WS row.

Next row: knit, inc into every 8th st (56 sts). Now change to No.6 needles and cont in st st, inc 1 st each end of every 4th row until you

have 110 sts. Work straight for 2 rows. Bind off loosely.

Collar

Using No.4 and main color, cast on 140 sts and work in seed st for 4in. Bind off in pattern.

Finishing

Knit one shoulder seam tog, bind off the 40 back neck sts, loosely, knit second shoulder seam tog (*see* Techniques, pages 13-14). Lay the work flat and pin the sleeves in position, taking care not to bunch or stretch them. Sew with a flat seam. Join the side and sleeve seams with a flat seam but start the side seams where the seed st band finishes so that there are 1¼in vents either side of the finished garment.

Join the side edges of the collar to a depth of ½in to make it stand very slightly, and place this seam to the center front of the neck. Attach around the neck with a flat seam.

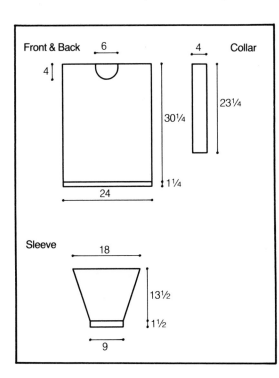

Front & Back — 6 — 4 — Collar

4

30¼

23¼

1¼

24

Sleeve — 18

13½

1½

9

CRUELLA DE VIL WOMEN'S DRESS

The evil Cruella, scourge of 101 Dalmatians, is featured on this turtle-neck dress, which uses both aran-weight wool and mohair for the motifs.

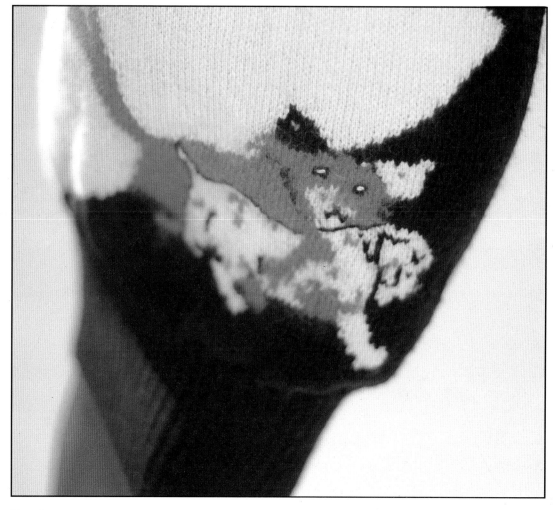

Materials
Yarnworks aran-weight wool – black: 16oz; white: 7oz; dark red and scarlet: 1¾oz each; grey, khaki and fawn: less than 1oz each. Yarnworks mohair – less than 1oz each of mink, brown, ginger, orange and turquoise, matched exactly to the charts. Silver ribbon: less than 1oz.

Needles
One pair of No.6 and one pair of No.8 needles; a set of double-pointed No.6 needles.

Gauge
Using No.8 needles and measured over st st: 18 sts and 23 rows = 4in square.
NOTE: To avoid puckering, keep your gauge the same when working the color motifs. Do not carry the main color behind the motifs.

Front
Using No.6 needles and black, cast on 74 sts. Row 1: *k1, p1, rep from * to end. Repeat this row to form single ribbing for 7¾in, ending on a RS row. Purl the next row, inc into every 3rd st (98 sts). Now change to No.8 needles and cont in st st, working from chart, ignoring the line running across Cruella, which relates to the back only. When the armhole point is reached, bind off 2 sts at beg of these 2 rows and cont to neck shaping point. **Shape neck:** work 34 sts, bind off 26 sts, work to end. Cont with this set of sts, leaving others on a holder. Now dec 1 st at neck edge on every row until 26 sts remain. Put sts on a holder. Return to the other set of sts, joining yarn in at neck edge. Shape to match. Leave sts on a holder.

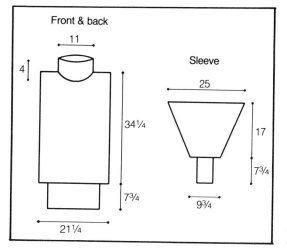

Front & back

11

4

34¼

7¾

21¼

Sleeve

25

17

7¾

9¾

The chart on pages 28 and 29 is for the front of the dress.

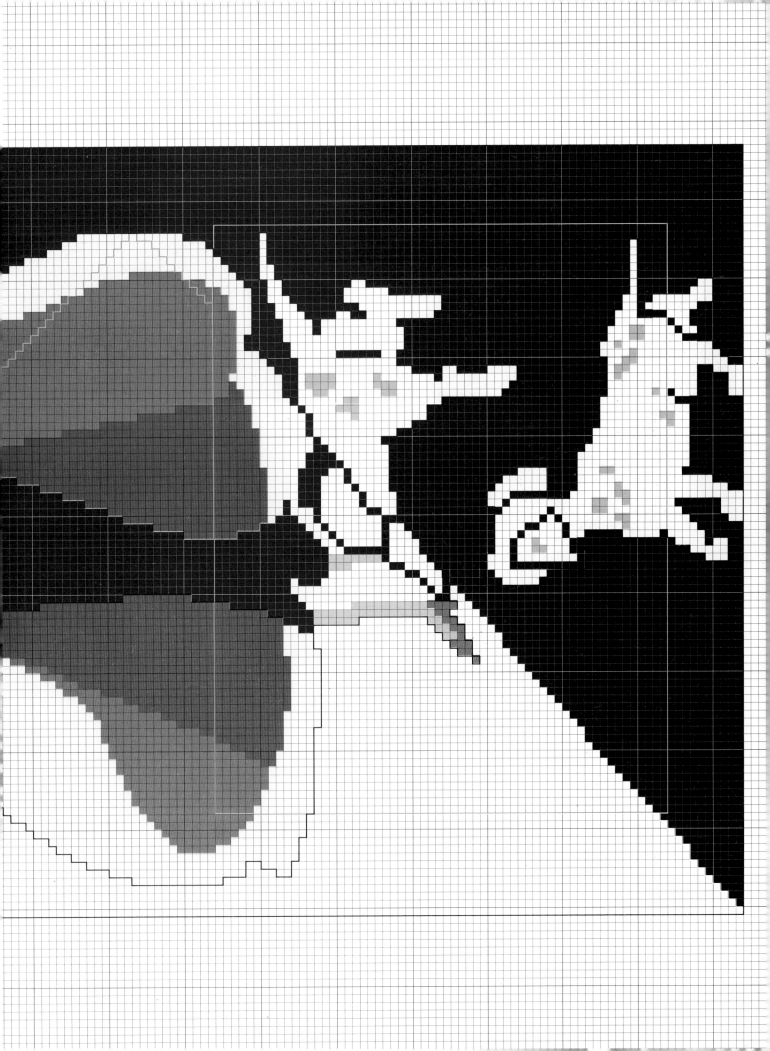

Back

Same as for the front but working plain st st in main colors only for 9 more rows, after the inc row (refer to backview photograph).

Row 11 (RS): k11, k the first row of cat chart, k to end. Cont working the chart in this position until it is complete. Now cont in st st in main colors only, following the dividing line, marked on chart but omitting Cruella. Shape armholes as on front. When 195 rows have been worked **shape neck**: work 31 sts, bind off 32 sts, work to end. Cont with this set of sts, leaving others on a holder. Dec 1 st at neck edge on every row until 26 sts remain. Leave sts on a holder. Return to the other set of sts, joining in yarn at neck edge. Shape to match first side. Leave sts on a holder.

Sleeves

Using black and No.6 needles, cast on 50 sts and work in single ribbing for 7¾in, ending with a WS row. Knit the next row, inc into the first and every following 5th st (59 sts). Now change to No.8 needles and cont in st st,

working from the sleeve chart (page 33). Work the dog only on the right sleeve and the smoke only on the left, and inc 1 st each end of every 5th row. When you have 95 sts cont straight to the length shown. Bind off loosely.

Neckband

Knit both shoulder seams tog (see Techniques, pages 13-14). Using double-pointed No.6 needles and black, knit up 48 sts around the back neck and 58 sts around the front. Knit the first row and then work in single ribbing for 4in. Bind off loosely, in ribbing.

Finishing

Lay the work flat and pin the sleeves in position, distributing them evenly, each side of the shoulder seams, and avoiding any bunching. Attach with a flat seam and then join side and sleeve seams likewise. Embroider the outline of the dog and the dog's eye and cat's eyes, as illustrated, using backstitch.

The cat chart should be incorporated only into the back of the dress.

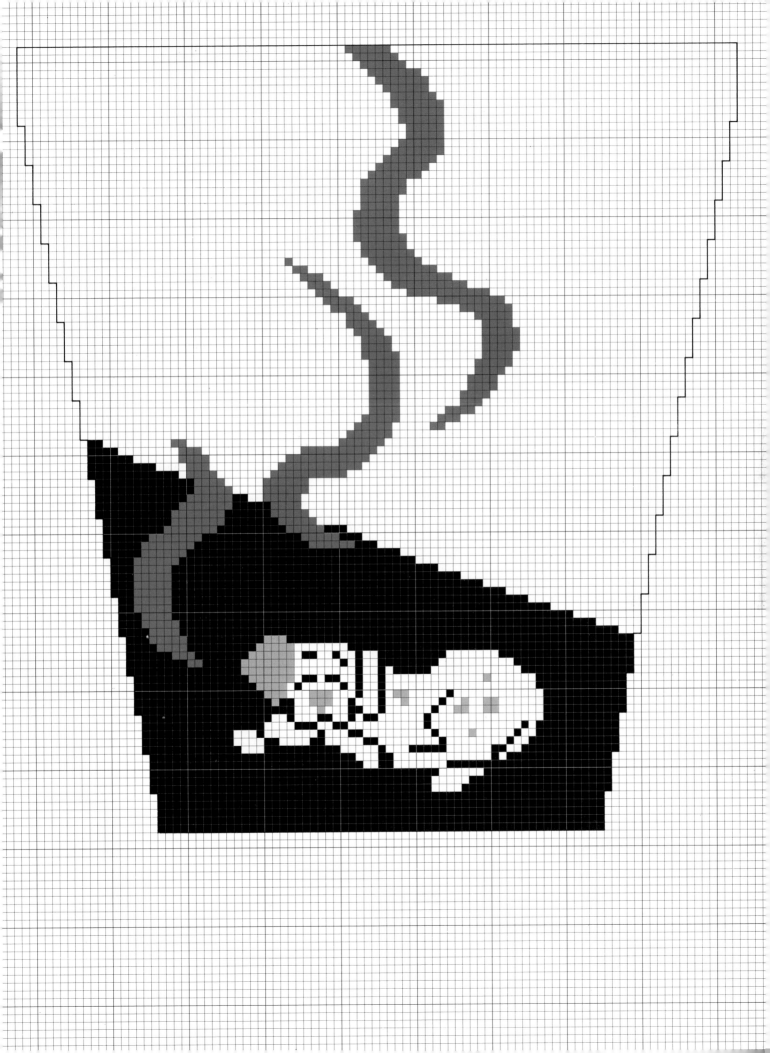

DAISY DUCK HAT, SCARF AND GLOVES SET

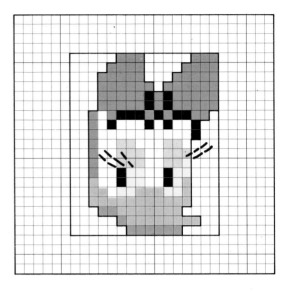

Materials

Main color: hat: 3½oz Yarnworks worsted weight yarn; scarf: 9oz Yarnworks worsted weight yarn; gloves: 2oz Yarnworks sport weight yarn. Contrast colors – less than 1oz of each color, matched exactly to the chart.

Needles

A set of double-pointed No.6 needles for the hat; one pair of No.6 needles for the scarf; a set of double-pointed No.4 needles for the gloves.

Gauge

Using worsted weight yarn, No.6 needles and measured over st st: 22 sts and 32 rows = 4in square; using sport weight yarn, No.4 needles and measured over st st: 28 sts and 36 rows = 4in square.

NOTE: To avoid puckering keep your gauge the same when working the color motif. Do not carry the main color behind the motif.

A warm combination of hat and scarf, worked in worsted weight wool, with gloves in sport weight. The colors of the motifs on the hat and gloves are echoed in the multi-colored fringes of the scarf.

HAT

Using double-pointed No.6 needles and main color, cast on 116 sts and work in rounds of single ribbing for 1½in. Now cont in st st, working straight until the work measures 3½in from the beg. Next round: k58, k the first row from the chart, k to end. Cont working the chart in this position until it is complete. Now cont in main color only. Work 2 rows straight and then divide the sts into 4 groups with a marker before every 29th st. These 4 sts are the axial sts. Dec 1 st each side of each axial st on the next round (8 sts in all), and every following 8th round until 66 sts remain. Now dec 1 st each side of each axial st on every 4th round until 6 sts remain. Work 4 more rounds and then thread the yarn through the remaining sts, draw them up and secure them on the inside of the hat.

SCARF

Using No.6 needles and main color, cast on 72 sts.
Row 1: *k1, p1, rep from * to end. Repeat this row to form single ribbing. Work straight until the scarf measures 55in. Bind off knitwise.

Fringes

The fringes are worked in the motif colors (excluding black) and are attached to the scarf alternately with main color fringes, giving a total of 20 fringes along each end (*see* Techniques, page 16).

GLOVES

Right hand

Using a set of double-pointed No.4 needles, cast on 42 sts and work in single ribbing for 2in. Next row: knit, inc into every 7th st (48 sts). Cont in st st. Work 4 more rounds. Now **work thumb gusset**: 5th round: k2, m1, k1, m1, to end. Work 3 more rounds. 9th round: k2, m1, k3, m1, k to end. Work 3 more rounds. 13th round: k2, m1, k5, m1, k to end. 14th round: k to last 18 sts of the round, work the first row of the

chart, k to end. Work the chart in this position until it is complete. Cont in main color only. Meanwhile cont inc 2 sts every 4th round as set, 6 times (60 sts).
Work 8 rounds without shaping. Divide for thumb: k1, slip the next 14 sts onto a thread, cast on 5 sts, k to end. Work 14 more rounds without shaping.

First finger: k8, slip next 37 sts onto a thread, cast on 2 sts, k last 6 sts (16 sts now on needle). Divide sts onto 3 needles and work 25 rounds or more, according to finger length required. Next round: k2 tog all around. Work 1 round without shaping and then draw yarn through remaining sts and secure.

Second finger: k the next 6 sts of the round, cast on 2 sts, k last 7 sts of round and knit up 2 sts from the base of the first finger where the 2 sts were cast on (17 sts). K approx 31 rounds, to suit. Shape tip as for first finger.

Third finger: k next 6 sts of round, cast on 2 sts, k last 6 sts of round, knit up 2 sts from the base of the 2nd finger (16 sts). Work as for first finger.

Fourth finger: k remaining 12 sts of the round, knit up 2 sts from the base of the third finger. Knit approx 21 rounds, to suit. Shape tip as for first finger.

Thumb: k 14 sts which had been held, knit up 5 sts from the cast on sts. Divide between 3 needles. Work approx 23 rounds, to suit. Shape tip as for first finger.

Left hand

Same as for right hand until the start of the thumb gusset: k to last 3 sts, m1, k1, m1, k2. Work 3 more rounds. 5th round: k to last 5 sts, m1, k3, m1, k2. Work 3 more rounds. Cont inc, as set, on next and every following 4th row until you have 60 sts, meanwhile placing the chart to correspond with that on the right hand. Work 8 rounds without shaping. **Divide for thumb**: k to last 16 sts, cast on 5 sts, slip next 14 sts onto a thread, k2. Work 14 rounds.

First finger: k first 6 sts of round, slip all but last 8 sts onto a thread, cast on 2 sts, k8 (16 sts). Work as for other hand.

Second finger: k the first 7 sts from the thread, cast on 2 sts, k to last 6 sts, knit up 2 sts from first finger (17 sts). Work as for other hand.

Third finger: k next 6 sts from the thread, cast on 2 sts, k to last 6 sts, knit up 2 sts from the second finger (16 sts). Work as for other hand.

Fourth finger: k remaining 12 sts, knit up 2 sts from third finger (14 sts). Work as for other hand.

DONALD DUCK TODDLERS' SAILOR SUIT

Materials

Yarnworks mercerized sport weight cotton –
sweater: blue: 6/7oz; red and yellow: less than 1oz of each color.
Hat: blue: 1¾oz; black: less than 1oz.
4 large "brass" buttons; approx 32in of black ribbon, ⅝in wide.

Needles

One pair No.2 and one pair of No.4 needles.

Gauge

Using No.4 needles and measured over st st: 28 sts and 36 rows = 4in square.

A replica of Donald Duck's sailor sweater and hat for toddlers. Worked in mercerized sport weight cotton, the sweater instructions are given for 18/24 months; the hat is one size.

SWEATER

Back

Using No.2 needles and main color, cast on 86/94 sts and work in garter st (knit every row) for 9 rows. Change to No.4 needles and cont in st st until work measures 12½/14½in. Leave sts on a spare needle.

Front

Same as for back until work measures 9¾/11¾in. **Divide for neck**: work 43/47 sts, turn work and leaving remaining sts on a holder. Dec 1 st at neck edge on every row until 22/24 sts remain. Work straight until it matches the back. Leave sts on a holder and return to other side of neck, joining yarn at neck edge and shaping to match the first side. Leave sts on a holder.

Sleeves

Using No.2 needles and main color, cast on 42/48 sts and work in garter st, inc 1 st each end

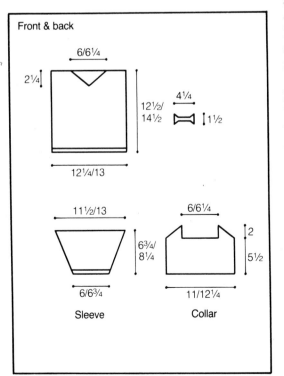

Front & back

6/6¼

2¼

12½/14½

4¼

1½

12¼/13

11½/13

6¾/8¼

6/6¾

Sleeve

6/6¼

2

5½

11/12¼

Collar

of the 3rd/6th row and every following 3rd row. When 8 garter st rows have been worked, change to No.4 needles and yellow and work in st st for 9 rows (cont to inc as before). Change back to main color and cont in st st, inc as before until you have 82/94 sts. Work straight until sleeve measures 6¾/8¼in. Bind off loosely.

Collar

Using No.2 needles and yellow, cast on 78/86 sts and work in garter st for 10 rows. Change to No.4 needles.
Next (RS) row: k7 yellow, join main color, k64/72, join a second ball of yellow and k7. Row 2: k7 yellow, p64/72 main color, k7 yellow. Rep these last 2 rows until the collar measures 5½in, ending with a WS row.
Next row: k7 yellow, k11/13 main color, bind off 42/46 sts, k11/13 in main color, k7 yellow. Cont with this set of sts, putting the other set onto a holder. Work 6/8 rows straight with the yellow border in garter st, as set.
Next (WS) row: k7 yellow, change to main color, p2 tog, p to end. Row 2: k to last 9 sts, k2 tog, change to yellow and k7. Repeat the last 2 rows until all main color sts have been decreased. Cont working the yellow border in garter st, keeping the neck edge straight, and at the same time dec 1 st at the outer edge on every row until all sts have been disposed of. Return to the other side of the collar, join yarn at neck edge and work as for the first side, reversing shapings.

Bow

Using No.4 needles and red, cast on 14 sts and work in garter st, dec 1 st each end of every 3rd row until 6 sts remain. Work straight for 2¼in and then inc 1 st each end of every 3rd row until you have 14 sts once again. Bind off.

Finishing

Knit one shoulder seam tog (*see* Techniques, pages 13-14), bind off the 42/46 back neck sts and then cont to knit tog the other shoulder seam. Lay work flat and pin sleeves into position, taking care not to bunch them. Join with a narrow backstitch. Join side and sleeve seams with a flat seam over the garter st and a narrow backstitch over the st st. Attach the collar with a flat seam so that the tips of its points just meet at the bottom of the neck V. Tie

the bow into a single knot in its middle – i.e., the edge that was knitted straight – to form a mock bow tie. Stitch this directly at the front of the neck, taking a few sts through the knot so that it will remain knotted. Attach the four buttons to the front, positioning them as in the photograph.

HAT

Using No.4 needles and black, cast on 80 sts. Row 1: * k1, p1, rep from * to end. Repeat this row to form single ribbing. Work 6 rows in all and then change to blue. Next row: knit, inc into every 8th st. Row 2: purl. Row 3: knit, inc into every 9th st. Cont as established to inc 10 sts every knit row until you have 180 sts. Work 5 rows without shaping.

Next row: *k16, k2 tog, rep from * to end. Row 2: purl. Row 3: *k15, k2 tog, rep from * to end. Cont as established to dec 10 sts every knit row until 10 sts remain.

Next row: p2 tog all along the row. Now draw the yarn up through the remaining sts and secure.

Finishing

Sew tog with a flat seam. Take the ribbon, fold it in half and attach it to the top edge of the ribbing at the seam point, as shown. Cut Vs out of the ribbon ends to finish.

MICKEY MOUSE TODDLERS' SUIT

The instructions for these sport weight cotton shorts and a long-sleeved T-shirt for little Mickeys are given for 18/24 months.

T-SHIRT

Back

Using black and No.2 needles, cast on 76/82 sts. Row 1: *k1, p1, rep from * to end. Repeat this row to form single ribbing for 1½in, ending with a WS row. Next row: knit, inc into every 12th/13th st (82/88 sts). Now change to No.4 needles and cont in st st, until work measures 7½/8½in. **Shape armholes**: bind off 3/4 sts at beg of next 2 rows. Now dec 1 st each end of every row until 70/72 sts remain. Work straight until the back measures 12¼/14¼in, ending with a WS row.

Shape neck and shoulders (see Techniques, page 8): k17/18, put these sts on a holder, bind off 36, work to last 5/6 sts, turn and p to last 2 sts, p2 tog. Next row: k2 tog, k to last 10/11 sts, turn work and p to end. Put these sts on a holder and return to the other side of neck. Join yarn at neck edge and work to match the first side, reversing shapings.

Front

Same as for back until the work measures 11/12¼in, ending with a WS row. **Shape neck**: k25/26 sts, bind off 20 sts, work to end. Cont with this set of sts, leaving others on a holder. Dec 1 st at neck edge on every row until 15/16 sts remain. Now work straight, until the front measures 12¼/14¼in, ending with a WS row. **Shape shoulder**: next row: k to last 5/6 sts, turn and p to end.
Row 3: k to last 10/11 sts, turn and p to end. Leave sts on a holder. Return to other side of neck, join yarn at neck edge and work to match the first side, reversing shapings. Leave sts on a spare needle.

Sleeves

Using No.2 needles cast on 42/48 sts and work in single ribbing for 1½in. Change to No.4 needles and cont in st st, inc 1 st each end of every 4th row until you have 70/76 sts. Work straight until the sleeve measures 8½/10¼in. **Shape sleeve cap**: bind off 3/4 sts at beg of next 2 rows. Now dec 1 st each end of every row until 60 sts remain. Bind off 10 sts at beg of next 4 rows. Bind off remaining sts.

Neckband

Knit the left shoulder seam tog (see Techniques, pages 13-14). Using No.2 needles and with RS of work facing, knit up 42 sts across the back of the neck, 16 sts down the left side of neck, 20 sts across the front and 16 sts up other side of neck (94 sts). Purl the first row and then cont in single ribbing until the band measures 1in. Bind off loosely in ribbing.

Finishing

Knit the second shoulder seam tog and join the neckband with a flat seam. Join the side and sleeve seams with a flat seam over the ribbing, a narrow backstitch over the st st. Set the sleeves into the armholes, distributing the fabric evenly. Pin, and sew with a narrow backstitch.

SHORTS

Back

Start at the lower edge of the left leg. Using No.3 needles and main color, cast on 46/50 sts. Row 1: *k1, p1, rep from * to end. Repeat this row to form single ribbing for ¾in. Now change to No.4 needles and cont in st st, inc 1 st each end of the first row. When work measures 3½/4in, ending with a WS row, **shape crotch**: next row: bind off 3 sts, work to end. Row 2: purl. **Row 3: k1, k2 tog, k to end.** Rep last 2 rows (43/47) sts. Leave these sts on a spare needle.
Work the right leg to match, reversing shapings and dec by k2 tog through backs of loops (tbl). Now slip the left leg sts onto the same needle, with crotch shapings to the middle of the row.
Next row (WS): purl. Row 2: k40/44, k2 tog tbl, k2, k2 tog, k to end (84/92 sts).
Work straight until work measures 9¾/10¾in.
Shape waist: Next row: work to last 10 sts, turn and repeat. 3rd row: work to last 20 sts, turn and repeat. 5th row: work to last 30 sts, turn and repeat. Break off yarn and slip all sts onto the same needle. Now work across all sts dec 1 st in every 10 sts (76/83 sts). Cont in st st for 16 rows more. Bind off.

Materials
Shorts: 4/6oz Yarnworks sport weight yarn. **Top**: 6/7oz Yarnworks sport weight yarn.
2 large black buttons; ¾in wide elastic for the shorts.

Needles
One pair No.2, one pair No.3 and one pair No.4 needles.

Gauge
Using No.4 needles and measured over st st: 28 sts and 36 rows = 4in square.

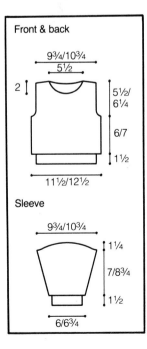

Front & back

9¾/10¾
5½
2
5½/6¼
6/7
1½
11½/12½

Sleeve

9¾/10¾
1¼
7/8¾
1½
6/6¾

Front

Work right leg as for back left leg until work measures 3½/4in, ending with a RS row.
Next row: purl. Row 2: work from ** to ** as for the back. Repeat these last 2 rows another 2 times more (45/49 sts). Leave these sts on a spare needle and work a left leg to match, reversing shapings and knitting 2 tog tbl. Cont as for back, but omit the short rows.

Finishing

Join seams with a flat seam, leaving the waist seam open for ¾in at the very top on one side. Turn in the bound-off edge and slip st it down inside the waist to form a tube ¾in deep. Thread elastic through the opening which has been left and join its ends according to waist size. Position the buttons as shown in the photograph.

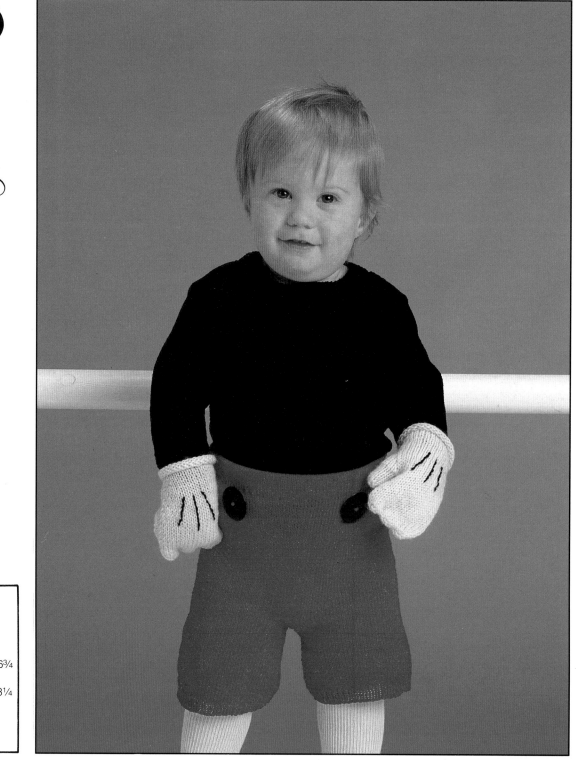

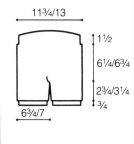

11¾/13

1½

6¼/6¾

2¾/3¼

¾

6¾/7

DONALD DUCK TODDLERS' FLIPPERS AND MICKEY MOUSE MITTENS

To complete the character outfits, here are Donald's flippers in sock form and Mickey's three-fingered gloves in mitten form. Both are worked in worsted weight wool. The two sizes are for 18/24 months.

FLIPPERS

(Make two)

Using a set of No.4 needles and yellow, cast on 28/32 sts. Place a marker on the needle at the beginning and work in rounds of k1, p1, ribbing for ¾in. Change to a set of No.6 needles and cont in st st until the sock measures 2¾/3½in. **Divide for heel**: halve the sts, leaving the back 14/16 sts (with the marker in the middle) on one needle and putting the instep sts on a thread to hold them. **Turn the heel**: keeping in st st, work back and forth on the heel sts, leaving an additional one unworked at the end of every row (*see* Techniques, page 8), until only 4 sts are being worked.

Cont to work in rounds again, placing the instep sts back on the needles. Work straight for 1½in from last turned row. Place 2 more markers 6/8 sts either side of the middle marker, which should now be removed. On the next round, inc 1 st (by working into the st on the row below the next st and then working the st itself) from the st after the first marker and inc another from the st before the 2nd marker. Cont inc 1 st at each of these positions on every other round until you have 44/48 sts on the needles (6/8 inc either side). Complete the round (to the point where the middle marker had been).

Next row: k5, bind off 12/14, k10 and leave these holding on one of the needles. Bind off 12/14, k to end of round and then 5 sts from the next round. Cont with these 10 sts on 2 needles. Row 2: p2 tog, p to last 2 sts, p2 tog through back loops (tbl). Knit the next row and then rep row 2. Work 0/1 row. Bind off. Return to the other 10 sts being held and work to match.

Finishing

Join the toe ends with a flat seam.

MITTENS

Left hand

Using a pair of No.6 needles and natural, cast on 26/28 sts and work in st st for 1¼in, ending with a WS row.

Next row: k1, inc 1 (work into the st on the row below the next one to be worked and then the st itself), k to last 2 sts, inc 1, k1. Work 3 rows straight and then rep inc row. Work 1 row straight.

Shape thumb gusset: Next row: k14/15, inc 1, k to end. Row 2 (and all WS rows): purl. Row 3: k1, inc 1, k12/13, inc 1 twice, k to last 2 sts, inc 1, k1. Row 5: k1, inc 1, k13/14, inc 1, k2, inc 1, k to last 2 sts, inc 1, k1 (39/41 sts). Now work the sides straight but cont to shape thumb gusset. Row 7: k16/17, inc 1, k4, inc 1, k to end. Row 9: k16/17, inc 1, k6, inc 1, k to end. Cont as established until you have 43/47 sts on the needle.

Next RS row: k16/17, slip the next 9/11 sts onto a thread, k to end, making sure that there is no stretched strand bridging the gap formed by the held sts. Work straight until the mitten measures 4¼/4¾in, ending with a RS row.

Shape top: p16/17, sl 1, p2 tog, psso. Row 2: k1, sl 1, k1, psso, k to last 2 sts, k2 tog. Row 3: p14/15, sl 1, p2 tog, psso, p to end. Row 4: rep row 2. Bind off tightly.

Work thumb: return to held sts and put them onto the set of double-pointed No.6 needles, inc 1 st from the base of the thumb. Work in rounds until it measures 1¼in from the first round. K2 tog all around next row and then draw yarn through remaining sts and secure.

Right hand

Same as for left hand but reversing the thumb gusset so that the first inc row reads: k16/17, inc 1, k to end.

Finishing

Join side and tops with a flat seam. On the RS, divide the tops into three and using natural yarn work a few very tight surface sts at the 2 points to create a slight indentation to give the impression of three fingers. Using black yarn, embroider the 3 black lines, as shown, using a small backstitch.

Materials

Flippers: 1¾oz of yellow Yarnworks worsted weight wool. **Mittens**: 1¾oz of natural Yarnworks worsted weight wool plus a small length of black wool for embroidery.

Needles

One pair of No.6 needles, a set of double-pointed No.6 needles and a set of double-pointed No.4 needles.

Gauge

Using No.6 needles and measured over st st: 24 sts and 32 rows = 4in square.

DUMBO TODDLERS' OUTFIT

A skirt suit with a raglan top for 2/3 year olds and a trouser suit with a drop-shoulder top to fit 1 year olds. Both incorporate the Dumbo motif, and the trouser suit is accompanied by Dumbo's hat and a striped scarf.

SKIRT

Knitted in one piece with a seam up the back. Using No.2 needles and main color, cast on 180 sts.
Row 1:*k2, p2, rep from * to end. Repeat this

Materials
Yarnworks sport weight wool – main color: raglan sweater: 8oz; skirt: 5oz; drop-shoulder sweater: 6oz; trousers: 6oz; hat: 1¾oz; scarf: 3½oz; contrast colors: less than 1oz of each color, matched exactly to the chart.
Both the skirt and trousers require elastic, 1in wide, length according to waist size. The drop-shoulder sweater requires 3 buttons.

Needles
One pair each of No.4, No.3 and No.2 needles; a set of double-pointed No.2 and a set of double-pointed No.4 needles for the raglan sweater collar and the hat.

Gauge
Using No.4 needles and measured over st st: 28 sts and 36 rows = 4in square.
NOTE: To avoid puckering, keep your gauge the same when working the color motif. Do not carry the main color behind the color motif.

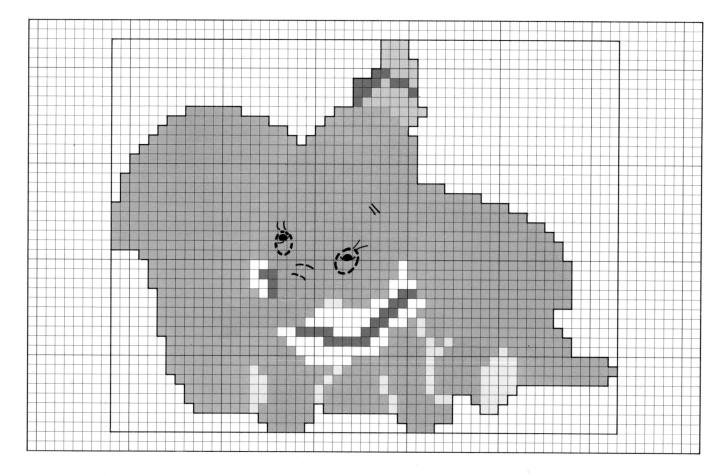

row to form double ribbing until the work measures 1½in, ending with a WS row. Next row: k, inc into every 22nd st (188 sts). Change to No.4 needles, purl the next row and cont in st st until the work measures 3½in, ending on a WS row. Next row: k51, work first row of chart, k to end. Cont working the chart in this position until it is complete. Now cont in main color until work measures 15¼in. Bind off.

Finishing

Sew the back seam with a flat seam, leaving 1in open at the top. Turn this depth in to form the waistband and sew down with slip stitch (*see* Techniques, page 13). Thread elastic through the waistband tube and join, end to end, according to waist size. Embroider Dumbo's eyes as illustrated (*see* Techniques, page 16).

RAGLAN SWEATER
Back

Using No.2 needles and main color, cast on 90 sts and work in double ribbing for 1in, ending on a WS row.
Next row: k, inc into every 22nd st (94 sts). Change to No.4 needles, purl the next row and cont in st st until work measures 6¼in. **Shape**

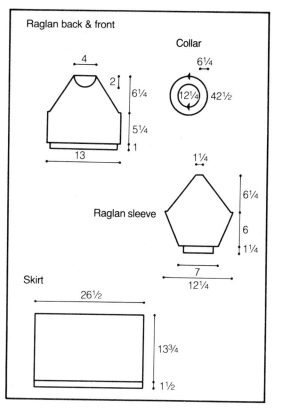

Raglan back & front

Collar

4

2

6¼

5¼

1

13

6¼

12¼   42½

Raglan sleeve

1¼

6¼

6

1¼

7

12¼

Skirt

26½

13¾

1½

raglan: bind off 4 sts at beg of next 2 rows. Dec 1 each end of the next and every other row until 28 sts remain. Work 1 row straight. Leave sts on a holder.

Front

Same as for back until 46 sts remain. Next row **shape neck**: work 16 sts, put remaining sts on a holder and turn work. Now dec 1 st each end of every other row until 3 sts remain. Work 1 row straight. Dec 1 st at raglan edge on next row. Work 1 row straight. Work 2 tog and pull yarn through final st to secure. Return to the other side of the neck, leaving the middle 14 sts on the holder. Shape to match first side.

Sleeves

Using No.2 needles and main color, cast on 44 sts and work in k2, p2 ribbing for 1¼in. Next RS row: k, inc into every 7th st (50 sts). Change to No.4 needles, purl the next row and cont in st st, inc 1 st each end of the next and every following 3rd row until you have 82 sts. Now inc 1 st each end of every other row until you have 88 sts. Work 2 rows straight. **Shape raglan**: bind off 4 sts at beg of next 2 rows and then dec 1 st each end of every other row until you have 30 sts. Now dec 1 st each end of every row until you have 10 sts. Leave sts on a holder.

Collar

Join the raglan seams with a very narrow backstitch. Using a set of double-pointed No.2 needles, main color and with the RS of work facing, knit up 13 sts down the left side of neck, knit the 14 middle sts onto a needle, knit up 13 sts up the right side of neck and then knit the right sleeve, back neck and left sleeve sts onto a needle (88 sts). Work in k1, p1 ribbing for 1in. Change to a set of No.4 needles and work in st st, remembering that the RS must be on the collar when it is turned back, as in the photograph.
Row 2: *k1, (knit into the st below the next one on the left-hand needle and then into the st itself) known as inc 1, rep from * to end of row (132 sts). Work 1 more row and then repeat the inc row (198 sts). Work 1 more row and then repeat the increase row once again (297 sts). Cont in st st until work measures 4in from the last row of ribbing, ending with a WS row. Now change to red and work 4 rows. Change back to main color. Work 2 more rows in st st. Change to No.2 needles and work 6 rows in garter st (since you are working in the round this must be worked as purl 1 row, knit 1 row). Bind off loosely, using a No.4 needle.

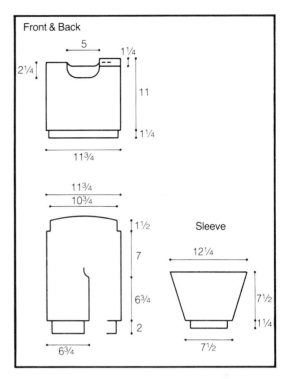

Finishing

Sew the side and sleeve seams with a flat seam on the ribbing, a narrow backstitch on the remainder.

TROUSERS
Back

Start at the lower edge of the left leg. Using No.2 needles and main color, cast on 36 sts. Row 1: *k1, p1, rep from * to end. Repeat this row to form single ribbing for 2in, ending with a WS row. Knit the next row, inc into every 3rd st (48 sts). Change to No.4 needles and cont in st st until work measures 8¾in, ending with a WS row. **Shape crotch**: next row: bind off 3 sts, work to end. Row 2: purl. Row 3: **k1, k2 tog, k to end.** Rep last 2 rows (43 sts). Leave these sts on a spare needle.
Work the right leg to match, reversing shapings and dec by k2 tog tbl. Now slip the left leg sts onto the same needle, crotch shapings to the middle of the row. Next row (WS): purl. Row 2: k40, k2 tog tbl, k2, k2 tog, k to end (84 sts). Work straight until work measures 15¾in.
Shape waist: Next row: work to last 10 sts, turn and repeat. 3rd row: work to last 20 sts, turn and repeat. 5th row: work to last 30 sts, turn and repeat. Break off yarn and slip all sts onto the same needle. Now work across all sts dec 1 st every 10th st (76 sts). Cont in st st for a further 16 rows. Bind off.

Front

Work right leg as for back left leg until work measures 8¾in, ending with a RS row.
Next row: purl. Row 2: work from ** to ** as for the back. Rep these last 2 rows twice more (45 sts).
Leave these sts on a spare needle and work a left leg to match, reversing shapings and knitting 2 tog tbl. Cont as for back, but omitting the turned rows.

Finishing

Join seams with a flat seam, leaving the waist seam open for 1in at the top on one side. Turn in the bound-off edge and sew down with slip st inside the waist to form a tube 1in deep. Thread elastic through the opening which has been left and join it, end to end, according to waist size.

DROP-SHOULDER SWEATER

Back

Using No.3 needles and main color, cast on 85 sts and work in k1, p1 ribbing for 1¼in. Change to No.4 needles and cont in st st until work

measures 11¼in. **Shape neck**: next RS row k26, bind off 33, k to end. Cont with this set of sts, leaving the others on a holder. Dec 1 st at neck edge on every other row two times. Change to No.3 needles and work remaining 24 sts in k1, p1 ribbing for 12 rows. Bind off in ribbing. Return to held sts, shape as for first side of neck and then cont straight in st st until work measures 12¼in from the beg. Leave sts on a spare needle.

Front

Same as for back until work measures 4in, ending with a WS row.

Next row: k15, knit the first row of chart, k to end. Cont working the chart in this position until it is completed. Now cont in main color until work measures 9¾in, ending with a WS row.

Shape neck: work 34, bind off 17, work to end. Cont with this set of sts, dec 1 st at neck edge on every row until 24 sts remain. Work straight until it measures 12¼in from the beg. Leave sts on a holder. Return to the other set of sts, and shape to match first side of neck. Now work straight until it measures 11⅝in from beg. Change to No.3 needles and cont in k1, p1 ribbing for 8 rows. On the next row **form buttonholes**: *rib 7 sts, bind off 1 st, rep from * once more and then rib to end. Rib next row, casting on 1 st above each st bound off on the previous row. Rib 2 more rows. Bind off in ribbing.

Neckband

Knit tog the left shoulder seam from armhole to neck (*see* Techniques, pages 13-14). Using a No.2 needle and with RS of work facing you, knit up 20 sts down the left side of the neck (starting at the top edge of buttonhole band), 17 sts across the front, 16 sts up the other side of the neck and 49 sts across the back neck, finishing at the edge of the buttonband (102 sts). Using No.3 needles, purl the first row and then rib 6 rows.

On the next row form a buttonhole: rib 2, bind off 1 st, rib to end. Rib the next row, casting on a st directly above that bound off on the previous row. Rib 3 more rows and then bind off loosely, in ribbing.

Sleeves

Using No.2 needles and main color, cast on 48 sts and work in k1, p1 ribbing for 1¼in, ending on WS. Next row: knit, inc into every 9th st (53 sts). Change to No.4 needles and cont in st st, inc 1 st each end of every 4th row until you have 87 sts. Work 1 row straight and then bind off loosely.

Finishing

Lay the work flat and pin the sleeves, avoiding bunching them. On the buttonband side, overlap the ribbing before attaching the sleeve. Stitch with a narrow backstitch. Join side and sleeve seams with a flat seam on the ribbing and a narrow backstitch for the st st. Attach buttons to correspond with buttonholes. Embroider Dumbo's eyes, as illustrated (*see* Techniques, page 16).

SCARF

Using No.4 needles and white, cast on 58 sts. Row 1: white *k1, p1, rep from * 5 more times, put yarn to back of work and join in red, twisting the strands to avoid a gap, (*see* Techniques, page 10), red **k1, p1, rep from ** twice more, put yarn to back of work and join in a second ball of white, twisting the strands as before. Rib to end.

Row 2: Rib in colors as set but twisting the yarns at the front of the work each time the color changes. Cont in ribbing, using three separate balls of yarn until work measures 27½in, ending on a WS row. Now bind off knitwise, using the first ball of main color yarn all the way across.

Finish off by attaching fringes of white yarn along cast on and bound-off edges (*see* Techniques, page 16).

HAT

Using double-pointed, No.2 needles and blue, cast on 116 sts and work in st st rounds for 5½in. Now work in single ribbing for 1in. Change to a set of No.4 needles and cont in st st, for 2in more, reversing the RS since the first band of st st is to be turned back on itself. Divide the sts exactly into 4 and place a marker at every 29th st. These 4 sts are the axial sts. Dec 1 st each side of every axial st on the next and every following 4th row until 12 sts remain. K2 tog all the way across the next round. Thread the yarn through the remaining sts, pull it tight and secure on the inside of the hat.

Finishing

Fold the band of st st in half, back on itself, so that the RS is facing and loosely sew down with slip stitch around the first row of the ribbing. Lightly press the fold into position.

FILMSTRIP FAIRISLE SWEATER

A drop-shoulder sweater for men and women in sport weight wool featuring Mickey and Minnie on celluloid and with a choice of V- or round-necks. The fairisle technique of color knitting is used throughout (*see* Techniques, page 9) and the instructions are given for women's/men's (see diagrams for actual measurements).

Back

Using No.2 needles and main color, cast on 150 sts.
Row 1: *k1, p1, rep from * to end. Repeat to form single ribbing for 2¼in, ending on a RS row. Purl the next row, inc into the first 2 and last 2 sts of the row (154 sts). Change to No.4 needles and start working from charts, keeping in st st throughout. Work the border chart and then 2 rows in main color only.
Chart 1: k1 in main color, k first row of chart working 4 repeats in all, k1 in main color. Work as set until the 27 rows are complete. *Now work 3 rows in main, followed by another border and then 2/4 rows in main.*
Chart 2: k4 in main color, k first row of chart working 10 repeats in all. Work as established until the 29 rows are complete. Now work from * to *
Chart 3: k4 in main color, k first row of chart, working 5 repeats in all. Work as established until the 28 rows are complete. **Now work 2/4 rows in main, followed by another border and then 2/4 rows in main.**
Chart 4: as for chart 3. Work from ** to **. Leave sts on a spare needle.

Front for V-neck version

Work women's as for back until 13 rows of chart 3 have been worked. Men's: work as for back until chart 3 is completed. Finish with 2/4 main color rows.
Divide for neck (meanwhile cont in pattern as for back): work pattern on 77 sts and turn work, leaving remaining sts on a holder. Cont with this set of sts, dec 1 st at neck edge on every row for 3 rows. Now dec 1 st at this edge on every other row until 53/52 sts remain. Work straight until the pattern has been completed, as on back. Leave sts on a holder. Return to the other side of the neck, join yarn at neck edge and shape to match the first side. Leave sts on a holder.

Front for round-neck version

Work as for back until 16 rows of chart 4 have been worked.
Row 17: work 66 sts, bind off 22 sts, work to end. Cont with this set of sts, keeping in pattern throughout, leaving others on a holder. Dec 1 st at neck edge on every row until 46 sts remain. Now work straight until the front matches the back. Leave sts on a holder. Return to other set of sts, join yarn at neck edge and shape to match first side. Leave sts on a holder.

Sleeves

Using No.2 needles and main color, cast on 56 sts and work in single ribbing for 3¼/4in, ending with a RS row. Next row: purl, inc into every 3rd st (74 sts). Now change to No.4 needles and start working the charts and main color rows in exactly the same sequence as on the back, working as many st repeats or edge repeats as will fit the number of sts. Meanwhile inc 1 st each end of every 4th row until you have 124 sts (working all new sts into color pattern as you go). Now inc 1 st each end of every 3rd row until there are 132/140 sts. Work straight until the border that follows chart 3 is complete. Bind off loosely.

Materials

Yarnworks sport weight wool – main color: 18/20oz; black: 4/4oz; red: 3/3oz; yellow: 1¾/1¾oz; white 3/3oz.

Needles

One pair of No.2 and one pair of No.4 needles.

Gauge

Using No.4 needles and measured over color pattern not main color st st: 28 sts and 28 rows = 4in square.

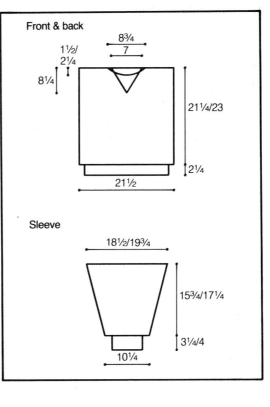

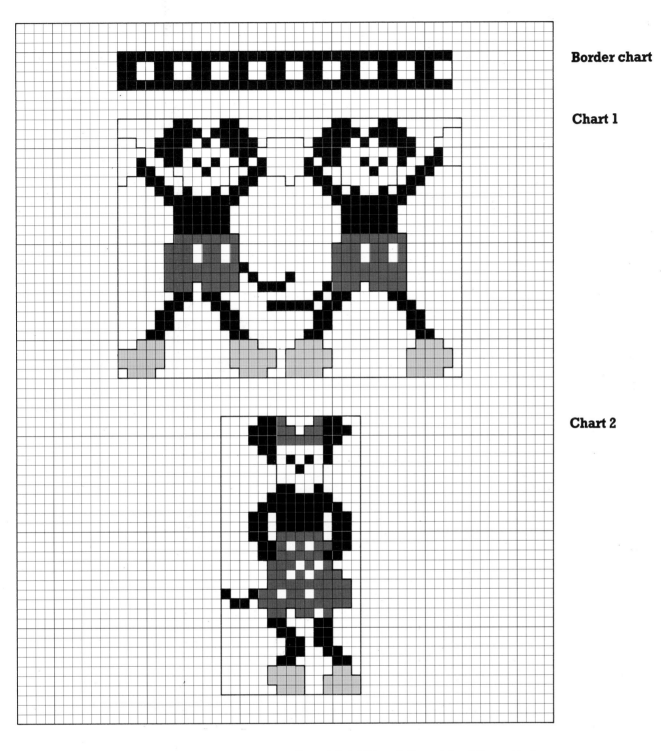

Border chart

Chart 1

Chart 2

V neckband

Knit the left shoulder seam together from armhole to neck edge (*see* Techniques, pages 13-14). Using No.2 needles, slip the 48/50 back neck sts on to one needle and then with the RS facing, knit up 64/66 sts down the left side of neck, 1 st from the strand where the neck was divided (this becoming the axial st), and 64/66 sts up the other side (177/183 sts). Purl the first row.

Next row: *k1, p1, repeat from * to 2 sts before the axial st, k2 tog, k the axial st, k2 tog, **p1, k1, repeat from ** to end.

Row 2: rib to 2 sts before axial st, k2 tog, p the axial st, k2 tog, **p1, k1, repeat from ** to end. Rep the last 2 rows until the border is 1¼in. deep. Bind off in ribbing.

Round neckband

Knit the left shoulder seam tog. Using No.2 needles, slip the 62 back neck sts onto one needle and then with RS facing, knit up 18 sts

Chart 3

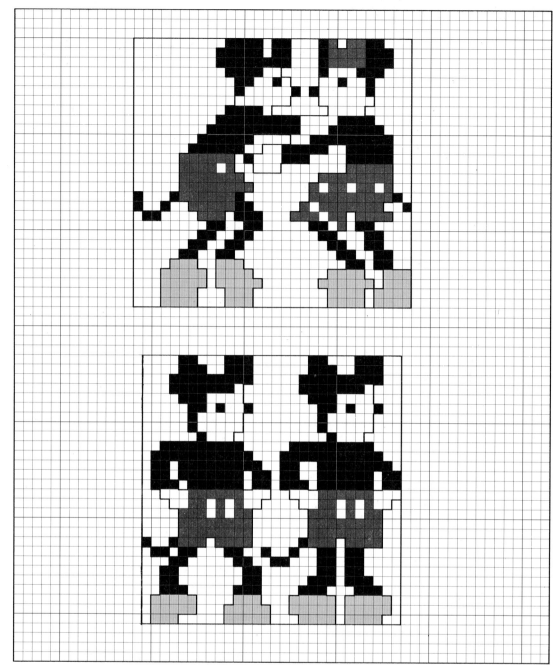

Chart 4

down the left side of the neck, 22 across the front and 18 up the other side (120 sts). Purl the first row and then work in single ribbing for 1¼in. Bind off loosely in ribbing.

Finishing

Knit right shoulder seam tog and join neckband with a flat seam. Lay work flat and pin the sleeves in position, taking care that they are not bunched or stretched. Attach with backstitch. Join all other seams with a flat seam across the ribbing and backstitch over the st st.

GOOFY JACKET

An oversized, bulky-weight jacket with a shawl neck and zipper. A giant Goofy motif is featured on the back panel, the red of his shirt being echoed in the stripe borders of all five pockets. With its drop shoulders and deep cuffs, this one-size jacket is suitable for men or women.

Materials
Yarnworks bulky wool – blue: 64oz; black: 6oz; red: 8oz; yellow: 4oz; white: 8oz. One 28in separating zipper. If you have trouble finding the right size separating zipper, special zippers can be ordered from Feibusch Zippers, 33 Allen Street, New York, NY 10002. Telephone (212) 226-3964. This store carries medium-weight, nylon separating zippers in a wide variety of colors for about $5 each. Inquire about price and shipping.

Needles
One pair of No. 10½ and one pair of No. 9 needles.

Gauge
Using No. 10½ needles and measured over st st: 14 sts and 19 rows = 4in square.
NOTE: To avoid puckering, keep your gauge the same when working the color motif. Do not carry the main color behind the motif.

Pocket linings

Worked in st st on No.10½ needles using blue. Leave each one on a spare needle until required.

For fronts (work 2): cast on 31 sts and work for 6¼in.

For breast pocket: cast on 25 sts and work for 5½in.

For sleeves (work 2): cast on 29 sts and work for 6in.

Back

Using No.9 needles and blue, cast on 92 sts. Row 1: * k2, p2, rep from * to end. Repeat this row to form double ribbing until it measures 2¾in, ending with a WS row.

Change to No.10½ needles and cont in st st, working the chart thus: row 1: k7, k the first row of the chart, k to end. Cont working the chart in this position until it is complete. Work 6 rows in main color only. Leave sts on a holder.

Right front

Using No.9 needles and blue, cast on 48 sts. Row 1: k4, * p2, k2, rep from * to end. Row 2: * p2, k2, rep from * to last 4 sts, k4.

Cont thus, in double ribbing with a 4 st garter st border, until the work measures 2¾in, ending with a WS row.

Change to No.10½ needles. Now cont in st st, except for the 4 border sts, which are cont in garter st throughout. When work measures 11in, ending on a WS row, **work pocket**: k8,

slip the next 31 sts onto a holder and work the 31 pocket lining sts instead, k to end of row. Cont as before until the work measures 24¾in, ending with a WS row. **Work breast pocket**: k8, slip the next 25 sts onto a holder and work the 25 pocket lining sts instead, k to end of row. Cont as before until work measures 28¾in, ending on a WS row. **Shape neck**: bind off 7 sts, k to end. Now dec 1 st at neck edge on every row until 36 sts remain. Now dec 1 st at neck edge on every other row until 33 sts remain. Work straight until front matches back. Leave sts on a spare needle.

Left front

Same as right front, reversing shapings and omitting the breast pocket.

Sleeves

Using No.9 needles and blue, cast on 40 sts and work in double ribbing for 4 rows. Change to red and rib 2 rows. Change back to blue and cont in ribbing until work measures 6in. Change to No.10½ needles and cont in st st, inc 1 st each end of next and every following 4th row until you have 68 sts. Next RS row **work pocket**: k19, slip the next 29 sts onto a holder and work the pocket linings sts instead, k to end. Cont shaping sleeve as before until you have 82 sts. Work straight until sleeve measures 23¼in. Bind off loosely.

Collar

Using No.10½ needles and blue, cast on 8 sts. Knit every row, inc 1 st each end of every other row, 1 st in from the edge, until you have 16 sts. Now work 1 edge straight while inc 1 st on every row on the other edge until you have 22 sts. Work straight for 72 rows. Now shape the other end to match, dec instead of inc until 8 sts are left. Bind off.

Pocket borders

Using No.9 needles and blue, work the held sts above each pocket in k1, p1 ribbing, starting with a RS row. Rib 2 rows blue, one row red and 1 more row blue. Bind off knitwise, in blue, taking care not to do so too tightly.

Finishing

Knit one shoulder seam tog (see Techniques, pages 13-14), bind off the 26 back neck sts and then knit the other shoulder seam tog. Slip stitch the side edges of the pocket borders to the main work, keeping them neat and straight. Pin the zipper into position so that the front edges of the knitting barely touch one another.

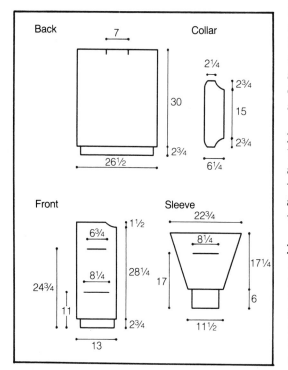

Using sewing thread, sew with slip st (*see* Techniques, page 13) the inner edges of the zipper to the inside of the knitting, taking care to work strong, firm sts which are not visible on the right side of the work.

Attach the collar to the neckline by its more shaped side, lining up the cast on/bound off edges of the collar with the bound off edges at the front of the neckline. Use a flat seam.

Lay the work flat and pin the sleeves to the body, avoiding bunching or stretching them. Attach with a flat seam. Join the side and sleeve seams similarly.

JUNGLE BOOK WOMEN'S SWEATER

A one-size sweater for women with a round neck and drop shoulders. Worked in mohair, it features the *Jungle Book* characters Baloo, King Louis and Kaa.

Materials
Yarnworks mohair – cream: 13½oz; jade: 2¾oz; emerald, silver, rust and chocolate: 1¾oz of each; less than 1oz of each of the other colors matched exactly to the charts.

Needles
One pair of No. 10 and one pair of No. 7 needles.

Gauge
Using No. 10 needles and measured over st st: 16 sts and 16 rows = 4in square.

The top chart on page 60 should be worked into the left sleeve, while the lower chart, Kaa, should be incorporated into the right sleeve.

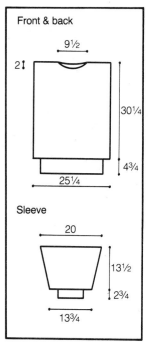

Front & back

9½

2↕

30¼

4¾

25¼

Sleeve

20

13½

2¾

13¾

Back

Using size No.7 needles and chocolate, cast on 88 sts.

Row 1: *k1, p1, rep from * to end. Repeat this row to form single ribbing for 4¾in, ending on a RS row. Purl the next row, inc into every 6th st (102 sts).

Change to No.10 needles and work from appropriate chart. Where marked on chart, **shape neck**: work 34 sts, bind off 34 sts, work to end. Cont with this set of sts, leaving others on a holder. Dec 1 st at neck edge on next 3 rows. Leave sts on a holder and return to other side of neck. Join yarn at neck edge and shape to match first side. Leave sts on a holder.

Front

Same as back but working from the appropriate chart. Where marked on chart, **shape neck**: work 39 sts, bind off 24 sts, work to end. Cont with this set of sts, leaving others on a holder. Dec 1 st at neck edge on every row until 32 sts remain. Work 1 row straight. Leave sts on a holder and return to other side of neck. Join yarn at neck edge and shape to match the first side. Leave sts on a holder.

Left sleeve

Using No.7 needles and jade, cast on 36 sts and work in single ribbing for 2¾in, ending with a RS row. Purl the next row, inc into every other st (54 sts). Change to No 10 needles and cont in

st st, working from the chart (page 60) and inc 1 st each end of the first and every following 4th row until you have 82 sts. Work 2 rows straight. Bind off loosely.

Right sleeve

Same as left sleeve but work the ribbing in silver and then work from the chart for the right sleeve (page 60).

Neckband

Knit the left shoulder seam tog (*see* Techniques, pages 13-14). Using No.7 needles, emerald and with RS facing, knit up 38 sts from around the back neck, 7 sts down the left front, 24 sts across the middle and 7 sts up the other side of neck (76 sts). Purl the first row and then work in single ribbing for 2¼in. Do not bind off but put the sts onto a thread.

Finishing

Knit the second shoulder seam tog and join the neckband edges with a flat seam. Turn the neckband in and slip st the held sts down to the point where they were originally picked up around the neckline (*see* Techniques, page 13). Lay work flat and pin the sleeves into position, distributing them equally either side of the shoulder seams; avoid bunching them. Join with a flat seam. Join side and sleeve seams likewise.

The top chart on page 60 should be worked into the left sleeve while the lower chart, Kaa, should be incorporated into the right sleeve.

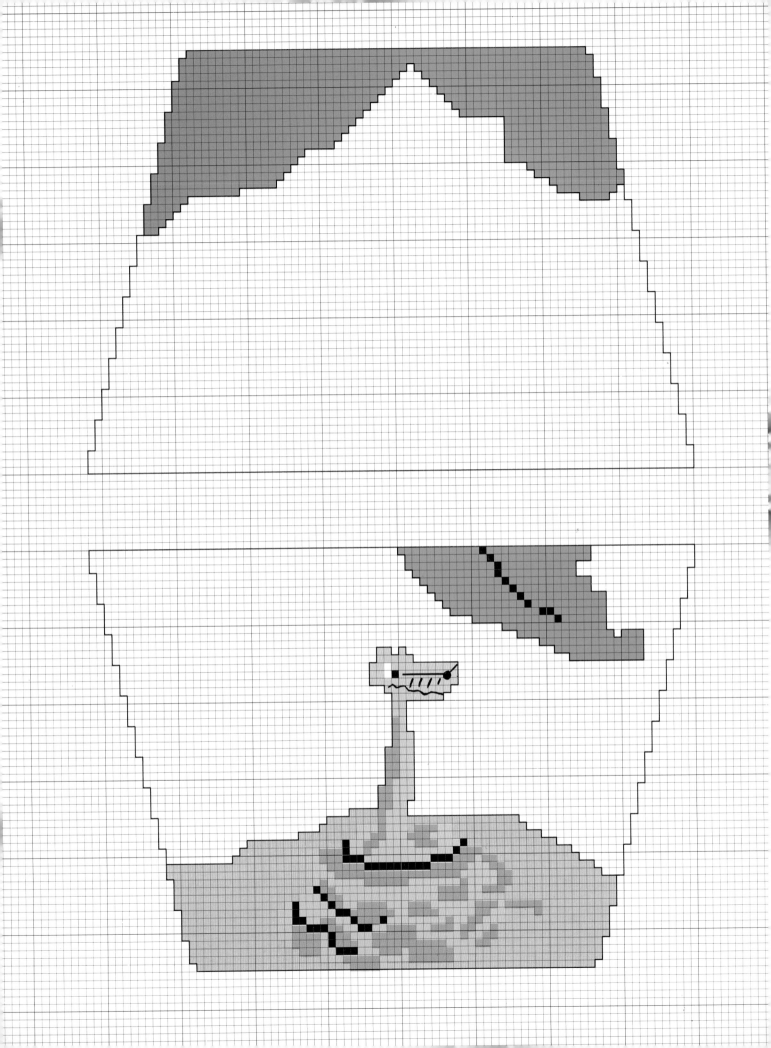

BULKY SWEATER FOR KIDS

A basic drop-shoulder, crew-neck sweater for 6/8/10 year olds, worked in bulky-weight wool. There is a choice of four character motifs: Minnie Mouse and Thumper may be worked on any size, but Donald Duck and the White Rabbit are for the two larger sizes only.

Back

Using main color and No.9 needles, cast on 48/52/56 sts.

Row 1: *k2, p2, rep from * to end. Repeat Row 1 to form double ribbing until it measures 2¼in, ending on a RS row. Next row: purl, inc into every 8th/8th/9th st (54/58/62 sts). Change to No.10½ needles and cont in st st until work

Materials

Yarnworks bulky wool – main color: 6 years: 20oz; 8 years: 22oz; 10 years: 24oz; contrast colors less than 2oz of each, matched exactly to the charts.

Needles

One pair of No.10½ and one pair of No.9 needles; a set of double-pointed No.9 needles.

Gauge

Using No.10½ needles and measured over st st: 14 sts and 19 rows = 4in square.
NOTE: To avoid puckering, keep your gauge the same when working the color motifs. Do not carry main colors behind the motifs.

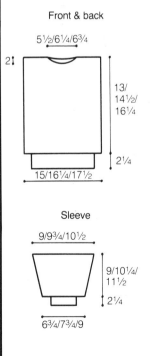

Front & back

5½/6¼/6¾

2↕

13/14½/16¼

2¼

15/16¼/17½

Sleeve

9/9¾/10½

9/10¼/11½

2¼

6¾/7¾/9

measures 15/16½/18in. **Shape neck**: work 19/20/21 sts, put 16/18/20 sts on a holder, work to end. Now cont working both sides of the neck simultaneously, joining a second ball of yarn at the first neck edge in order to do so. Dec 1 st at both neck edges on the next two rows. Leave sts on a spare needle.

Front

Same as back until the ribbing is completed and the increase row has been worked.
Row 2: change to No. 10½ needles and k 0/2/4, work chosen chart sts, k to end. Work chart in this position until it is complete. Now cont in main color until the work measures 13½/15/16½in. Next RS row **shape neck**: work 22/23/24 sts, put 10/12/14 sts on a holder, work to end. Now dec 1 st at both neck edges on every row (working both sides simultaneously as for back), until 17/18/19 shoulder sts remain each side. Now work straight until the front matches the back. Leave sts on a spare needle.

Sleeves

Using No.9 needles and main color, cast on 24/28/32 sts and work in double ribbing for 2¼in. Change to No. 10½ needles and cont in st st, inc 1 st each end of next 4th/1st/5th row and every following 4th/5th/5th row until you have 44/48/52 sts. Work straight until sleeve measures 11¼/12½/13¾in. Bind off loosely.

Neckband

Knit both shoulder seams tog (*see* Techniques, pages 13–14). Using double-pointed No.9 needles, main color and with RS of work facing you, pick up and knit 12 sts around the left side of the neck, knit the 10/12/14 front neck sts onto the needle, pick up and knit 12 sts around the right side of the neck and then knit the 16/18/20 back neck sts onto the needle (50/54/58 sts). Work in double ribbing for 1in. Bind off in ribbing.

Finishing

Lay the work flat and pin the sleeves to the body, avoiding bunching or stretching them. Attach with a flat seam. Join the neckband, side and sleeve seams with a flat seam.

STARS AND STRIPES MEN'S SWEATER

Materials

Yarnworks worsted weight cotton – main color: 36oz; red: 9oz; white: 7oz; pink: 1¾oz; black: 1¾oz; silver ribbon: 3½oz.

Needles

One pair of No.4 and one pair of No.5 needles.

Gauge

Using No.5 needles and measured over st st: 24 sts and 30 rows = 4in square.
NOTE: Use intarsia method of working, not fairisle (*see* Techniques, page 9).

A man-size Mickey Mouse sweater with a slash neck and drop shoulders worked in crisp worsted weight cotton with lurex stars.

Front

Using No.4 needles and blue, cast on 120 sts. Row 1: *k1, p1, rep from * to end. Repeat this row to form single ribbing for 4in, ending with a RS row. Next row: purl, inc into first and every following 7th st (138 sts). Change to No.5 needles and cont in st st, working the 36 rows of the stars and stripes border. Now change back to blue and work 4 more rows.

Next row: k34, k the first row of the Mickey chart, k to end. Cont working the chart in this position until it is complete. Work 3 more rows in blue only and then start working the stripe border, omitting the stars. Work 8 rows. Cont in stripe pattern but incorporate a single-ribbed neck border thus: next row: k39, rib 60, k to end. Cont with stripes but keep the ribbing in red throughout. When 18 stripe rows have been worked, leave sts on a holder.

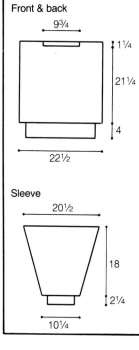

Front & back

9¾

1¼

21¼

4

22½

Sleeve

20½

18

2¼

10¼

64

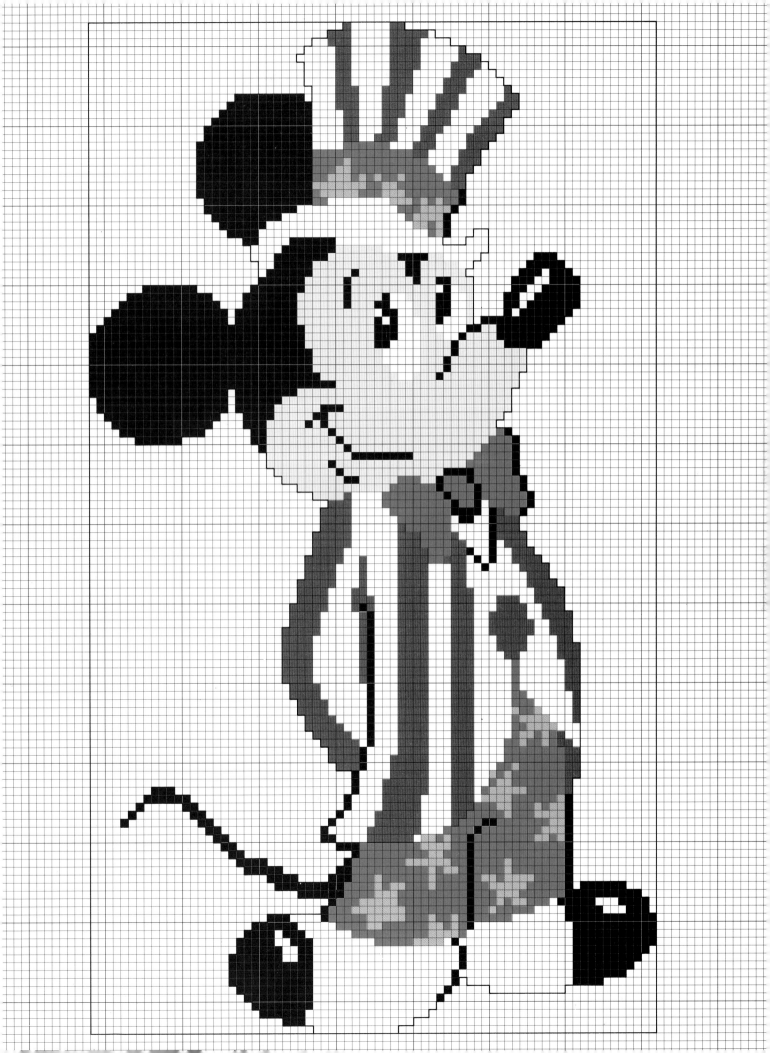

Back

Same as front, working the stars and stripes bands but omitting the Mickey chart. Work the same number of rows in plain blue.

Sleeves

Using No.4 needles and blue, cast on 56 sts and work in single ribbing for 2¼in, ending with a RS row.

Next row: purl, inc into every 9th st (62 sts).

Change to No.5 needles and cont in st st working the stars and stripes chart, vertically, as a central panel so that the first row reads: blue k13, k first row of chart, blue k to end. Cont with panel centered, inc 1 st each end of every 4th row until there are 126 sts.

Now work straight until 2 rows short of the end of the chart. Bind off firmly but not too tightly, using the relevant color for each area.

Finishing

Knit one shoulder seam together (*see* Techniques, pages 13-14). Bind off the front border ribbed sts and then knit the other shoulder seam tog. Bind off back neck border. Lay the work flat and pin the sleeves in position, taking great care to line up the stripes (the body stripes may need a light press to ensure that they correspond exactly with the sleeve stripes). Join with a flat seam, then join the side and sleeve seams likewise.

The stars and stripes chart should be worked vertically for the sleeves and horizontally, left to right, on the front and back of the sweater.

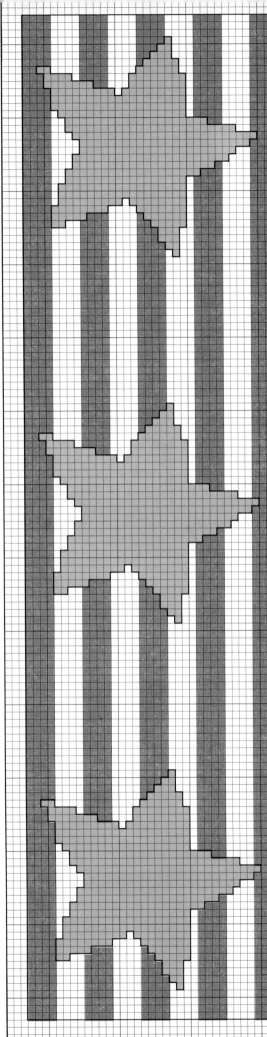

MICKEY MOUSE KIDS' JACKET

A miniature version of the over-sized Goofy jacket shown on page 51. Scaled down for 3/4 year olds, this jacket features Mickey Mouse on the back panel.

Pocket linings

Worked in st st on No. 10½ needles using blue. Leave each one on a spare needle until required.
For fronts (work 2): cast on 12 sts and work for 2¼in.
For sleeves (work 2): cast on 15 sts and work for 2¼in.

Back

Using No.9 needles and blue, cast on 52 sts. Row 1: *k2, p2, rep from * to end. Repeat this row to form double ribbing. Work 2 rows in blue, 2 rows in red and then cont in blue until work measures 2¼in, ending with a RS row. Change to No. 10½ needles and purl the next row, inc into every 13th st (56 sts). Next row: k2, k the first row of the chart, k2. Cont working the chart in this position until it is complete. Now cont in main color only until work measures 17¼in, ending with a WS row.
Shape neck and shoulders: k19 sts, bind off 14 sts, k to end. Cont with this set of sts, leaving the others on a holder. P2 tog at neck edge on next row.
Row 2: k to last 9 sts, turn and p to end. Leave these sts on a holder and return to the others, joining yarn in at outer edge. K2 tog at neck edge on next row. Row 2: p to last 9 sts, turn work and k to end. Leave sts on a holder.

Right front

Using No.9 needles and blue, cast on 28 sts. Row 1: k4, *p2, k2, rep from * to end. Row 2: *p2, k2, rep from * to last 4 sts, k4. Cont thus, in double ribbing, as for back, with a 4 st garter st border, ending with a WS row.
Change to No.10½ needles and cont in st st, inc 1 st at end of the first row and maintaining garter st border.
When work measures 5½in, ending on a WS row, **work pocket**: k8, slip the next 12 sts on to a holder and work the 12 pocket lining sts instead, k to end of row. Cont as before. When work measures 12½in, ending with a WS row, **work breast pocket**: as for first pocket. Cont as

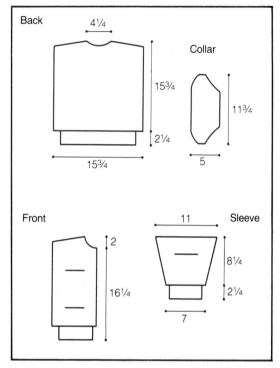

before until work measures 16¼in, ending on a WS row.
Shape neck: bind off 6 sts, k to end. Now dec 1 st at neck edge on every row until 18 sts remain. Work straight until front measures 17¾in, ending with a WS row. **Shape shoulder**: k to last 9 sts, turn and p to end. Leave sts on a holder.

Left front

Same as right front, reversing shapings and omitting the pockets.

Sleeves

Using No.9 needles and blue, cast on 24 sts and work in double rib for 2 rows. Change to red and rib 2 rows. Change back to blue and rib until work measures 2¼in.
Change to No.10½ needles and cont in st st, inc 1 st each end of next and every following 5th row until you have 36 sts. Next RS row **work pocket**: k11, slip the next 15 sts onto a holder and work the pocket lining sts instead, k to end. Cont shaping sleeve as before until you have 40 sts. Work straight until sleeve measures 10½in. Bind off loosely.

Materials

Yarnworks bulky-weight wool – blue: 18oz; black: 1¾oz; red: 1¾oz; white: 1¾oz; gold and royal blue: less than 1oz of each.
One 16in separating zipper.

Needles

One pair of No.10½ and one pair of No.9 needles.

Gauge

Using No.10½ needles and measured over st st: 14 sts and 19 rows = 4in square.
NOTE: To avoid puckering, keep your gauge the same when working color motif. Do not carry the main color behind the mofit.

67

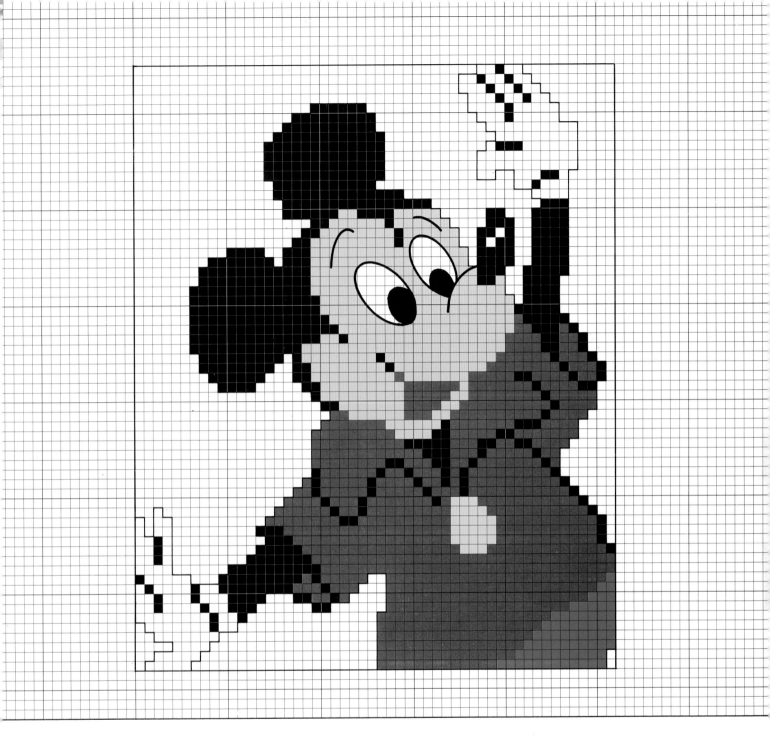

Collar

Using No.9 needles and blue, cast on 4 sts. Knit every row, inc 1 st each end of every other row, one st in from the edge, until you have 12 sts. Now work 1 edge straight while inc 1 st on every row on the other edge until you have 18 sts. Work straight for 30 rows. Now shape the other end to match, dec instead of inc until 4 sts are left. Bind off.

Pocket borders

Using No.9 needles and blue, work the held sts above each pocket in k1, p1 ribbing, starting with a RS row. Rib 1 row blue, one row red and 1 more row blue. Bind off knitwise, in blue, taking care not to do so too tightly.

Finishing

Knit both shoulder seams tog (*see* Techniques, pages 13-14). Sew with slip stitch the side edges of the pocket borders to the main work, keeping them neat and straight.

Pin the zipper into position so that the front edges of the knitting barely touch one another. Using sewing thread, sew with slip st the inner edges of the zipper to the inside of the knitting, taking care to work strong, firm sts that are not visible on the right side of the work.

Attach the collar with a flat seam, matching the bound off and cast on edges with the garter st front bands.

Lay the work flat and pin the sleeves to the body, taking care not to bunch or stretch them. Attach with a flat seam. Join the side and sleeve seams similarly.

Embroider the facial features as shown, using backstitch and satin stitch.

PLUTO MEN'S OR WOMEN'S SWEATER

A bulky-weight, roll-neck sweater for women or men. Pluto appears on the front, his bone on the back. The fit is very over-sized for women but a more standard fit for men (see diagrams for the actual measurements). The instructions are the same for women and men, except for the sleeves, which are quoted for women/men.

Back

Using No. 10½ needles and main color, cast on 88 sts.
Row 1: join *natural k2, main color p2, rep from * to end, loosely carrying the color not in use at the back of the work. Row 2: *main color k2, natural p2, rep from * to end, loosely carrying

color not in use at the front of the work. These 2 rows form the 2-tone double ribbing pattern. Work 2¼in in ribbing, ending with a WS row. Next row: using main color only, k1, inc 1, k to last 3 sts, inc 1, k to end. Cont in st st, until work measures 10¼in, ending with a WS row. Next row: k18, k first row of bone chart, k to end. Cont working the chart in this position until it is complete. Cont in main color until work measures 31½in. Leave sts on a spare needle.

Front

Same as back until you have worked the first 2 rows in st st.
Next row: k3, k from first row of Pluto chart, k to

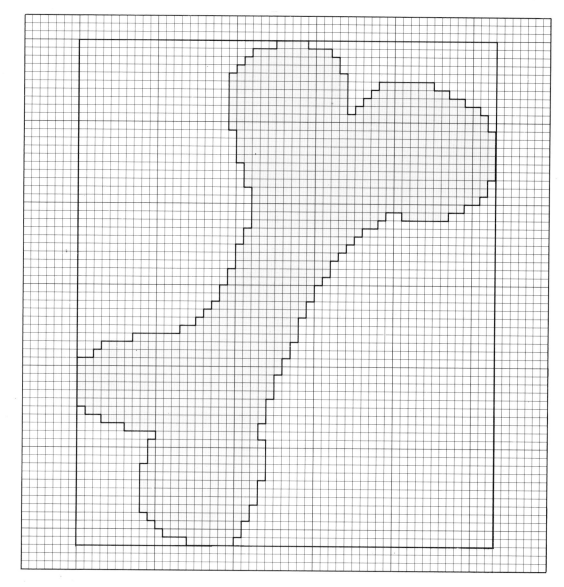

Materials
Yarnworks bulky-weight wool – blue: 50/54oz natural: 6oz; beige: 8oz; contrast: ¾oz of each of the four colors, matched exactly to the charts.

Needles
One pair of No. 10½ needles and a set of double-pointed No. 10½ needles.

Gauge
Using No. 10½ needles and measured over st st: 14 sts and 19 rows = 4in square.
NOTE: To avoid puckering keep your gauge the same when working the color motifs. Do not carry the main color behind the motif.

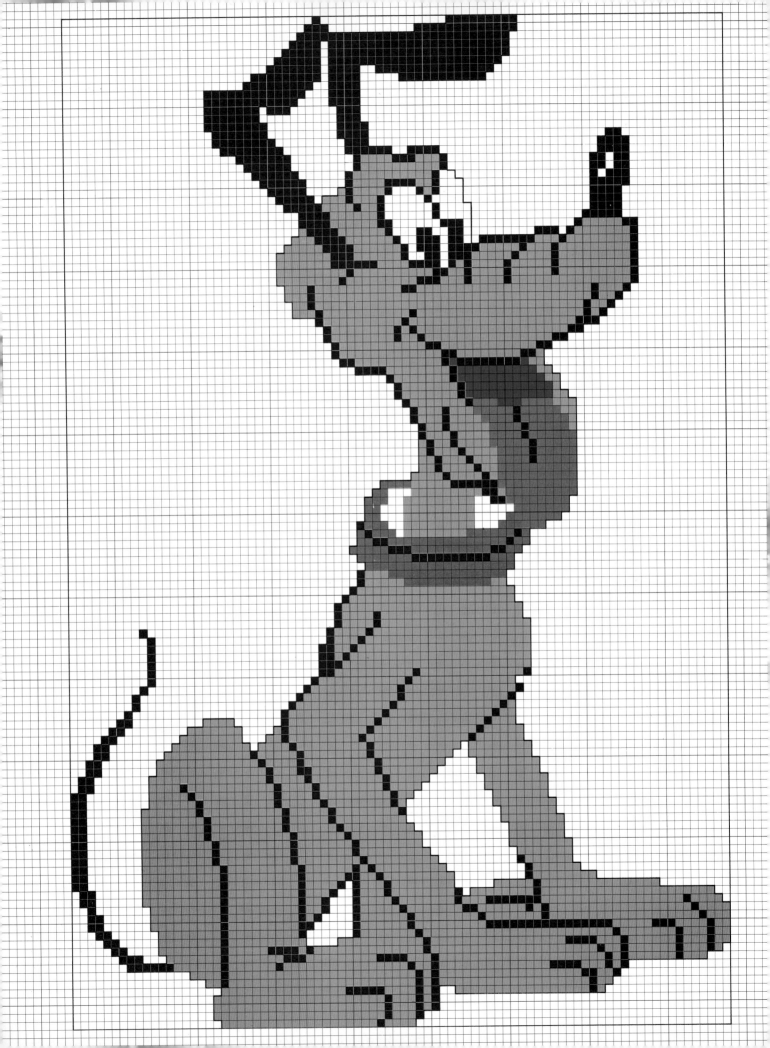

end. Cont working the chart in this position until it is complete. Work 2 rows in main color and then **shape neck**: work 40 sts, bind off 10 sts, work to end. Cont with this set of sts, leaving the others on a holder. Dec 1 st at neck edge on every row until 31 sts remain. Work straight until this side is as long as the back. Leave sts on a holder. Return to the other side of the neck and shape to match. Leave sts on a holder.

Sleeves

Using No. 10½ needles, cast on 28/32 sts and work in 2-tone double ribbing for 2in, ending with a WS row. Next row: knit in main color, inc 4 sts evenly along the row from sts worked in main color on the previous row (32/36 sts). Cont in main color and st st, inc 1 st each end of next and every following 4th/5th row until you have 70 sts. Work straight until sleeve measures 16¼/19¼in from beg. Bind off loosely.

Roll neck

Knit one shoulder seam tog, loosely bind off the 28 back neck sts, knit 2nd shoulder seam tog (*see* Techniques, pages 13-14). Using double-pointed No. 10½ needles, main color and with RS facing, knit up 11 sts down the left side of the neck, 10 sts across the front, 11 sts up the other side and 28 sts across the back (60 sts). Work in rounds of double ribbing for 4¾in. Join natural and purl the next row. Now rib 1 row and change back to main color. Purl 1 row and then cont in ribbing for 2 more rows. Bind off in ribbing.

Finishing

Join all seams with a very neat flat seam.

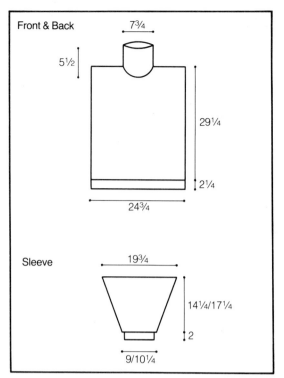

SNOW WHITE WOMEN'S PULLOVER

A round-necked, sleeveless sweater worked in sport weight wool, which may be worn as a twin set with the Seven Dwarfs Cardigan. The instructions are given for two sizes throughout, petite/small-medium (see diagram for actual measurements).

Back

Using No.2 needles and main color, cast on 112/120 sts.

Row 1: *k1, p1, rep from * to end. Repeat this row to form single ribbing until work measures 3in. Next WS row, purl, inc into every 11th/12th st (122/130 sts).

Change to No.4 needles and knit the next row. Row 3: p21/25. MB (see Techniques, page 11), p79, MB, p to end. Work 3 rows in st st. Repeat these 4 rows, keeping the bobbles in two straight lines for the entire length of the garment.

When 5/7 bobble rows have been completed, work 3 more rows in st st then work a horizontal band of bobbles thus: p5, *MB, p3, rep from * to last st, p1. Work another 55 rows (cont to work vertical bobble lines throughout), and then repeat the horizontal bobble band row. When work measures 13¾/14¾in, **shape armholes**: bind off 5 sts at beg of next 2 rows and then dec 1 st each end of every row until 102/110 sts remain. Now work straight to 55 rows from the previous bobble band. Next row: p3, *MB, p3, rep from * to last 3 sts, MB, p2. Cont to work straight until work measures 20½/21½in. Stop working the bobbles, cont in st st and **shape shoulders** (see Techniques, page 8).

Rows 1 and 2: work to last 10/12 sts, turn. Rows 3 and 4: work to last 19/22 sts, turn. Rows 5 and 6: work to last 28/32 sts, turn. Leave all sts on a spare needle.

Front

Work as for back until 8 rows have been worked after the first horizontal band of bobbles. Next row: k34/38, knit the first row from the chart, k to end. Cont working chart in this position until it is complete, meanwhile working the bobble grid around it – i.e., the grid forms a frame, the second horizontal band of bobbles stopping short of the first vertical line and starting up again the other side of the second vertical line so that it does not interfere with the motif.

Shape armholes: as for back and then work straight until the work measures 18½/19¼in, ending on a WS row.

Shape neck: k 41/45 sts, bind off 20 sts, work to end. Cont with this last set of sts, leaving the others on a holder. Dec 1 st at neck edge on every row until 34/38 sts remain. Now dec 1 st at this edge on every other row until 28/32 sts remain. Work straight until work measures 20½/21½in, ending with a WS row. Stop working bobbles and cont in st st. Next row **shape shoulder**: work to last 10/12 sts, turn and work to end. Row 3: work to last 19/22 sts, turn and work to end. Leave sts on a holder. Return to the other side of the neck and work to match, reversing shapings.

Neckband

Knit the left shoulder seam tog (see Techniques, pages 13-14). Using No.2 needles, slip the 46 sts at the back of the neck on to a needle and then, with RS of work facing, knit up 20/22 sts down the side of the neck, 20 across the front and 20/22 back up the other side (106/110 sts). Purl the first row, then work in single ribbing for 1¼in. Bind off loosely in ribbing.

Armbands

Knit together the right shoulder and lay the work flat. Using No.2 needles and with RS facing, knit up 104/112 sts evenly along the left armhole from front to back. Purl the first row and then work in single ribbing for 1¼in. Bind

Materials

Yarnworks sport weight wool – green: 8/9oz; contrast colors: less than 1oz of each of the 10 colors, matched exactly to the chart.

Needles

One pair of No.4 and one pair of No.2 needles.

Gauge

Using No.4 needles and measured over stockinette st: 28 sts and 36 rows = 4in square.

NOTE: To avoid puckering, keep your gauge the same when working the color motif. Do not carry the main color behind the motif.

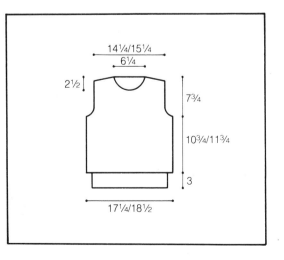

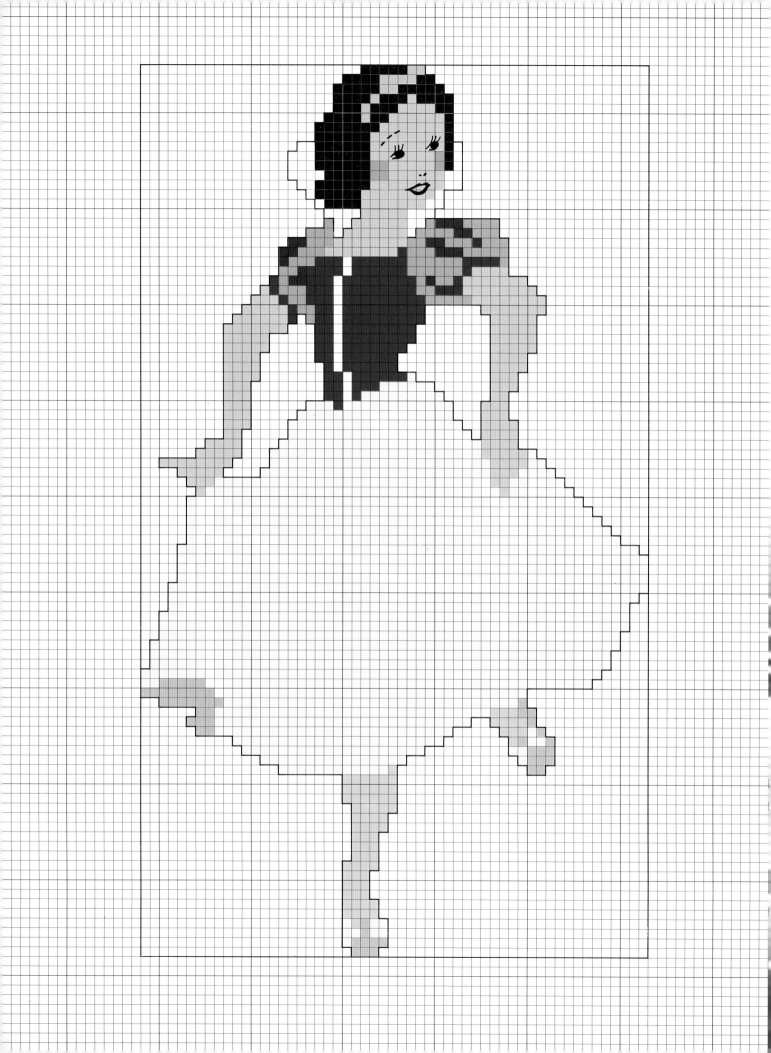

off loosely in ribbing. Work the right armband the same, knitting up the sts from the back to the front.

Finishing

Use a flat seam for all ribbed edges, a narrow backstitch elsewhere. Embroider Snow White's facial features as shown.

SEVEN DWARFS WOMEN'S CARDIGAN

Materials

Green: 15/16oz; contrast colors: less than 1oz of each of the 15 colors, matched exactly to the charts. 8 buttons.

Needles

One pair of No.4 and one pair of No.2 needles.

Gauge

Using No.4 needles and measured over st st: 28 sts and 36 rows = 4in square.
NOTE: To avoid puckering, keep your gauge the same when working the color motifs. Do not carry the main color behind the motifs.

A round-necked, set-in-sleeved 1940s-style cardigan, featuring the Seven Dwarfs in a grid of bobbles. Six dwarfs are worked on the front, with Bashful hiding on the back. The cardigan, which is knitted in sport weight wool, is given in two sizes, petite/small-medium.

Back

Using No.2 needles and main color, cast on 118/126 sts.
Row 1: *k1, p1, rep from * to end. Repeat this row to form single ribbing until work measures 4in. Next RS row: knit, inc into every 10th/11th st (129/137 sts). Change to No.4 needles and cont in st st, working the grid of bobbles from the chart but omitting the dwarfs except for Bashful, who should be worked in the same position as Grumpy is on the front.
After working the 3rd horizontal band of bobbles, work 4 more rows and then **shape armholes**: bind off 5 sts at beg of next two rows. Dec 1 st at each end of every row, 5 times (109/117 sts). Cont to work straight until the 4th horizontal row of bobbles has been completed. Work 12/18 more rows. Leave sts on a spare needle.

The symbol "X" on the charts on pages 80 and 81 indicates that bobbles should be worked at those points; *see* Making a bobble, page 11.
The inner line on the charts is for petite size, the outer line for the small–medium size.

Right front

Using No.2 needles and main color, cast on 57/61 sts and work in single ribbing for 4in. Next RS row: knit, inc into every 10th/11th st (62/66 sts). Change to No.4 needles and work from chart. After the 3rd horizontal row of bobbles, work 3 more rows and then **shape armhole**: bind off 5 sts at beg of next row and then dec 1 st at this edge on every row for 5 rows (52/56 sts). Work straight to the point where the neck shaping is indicated on the chart. Next RS row **shape neck**: bind off 5 sts, work to end. Now dec 1 st at neck edge on every row until 32/36 sts remain. Work straight until the front matches the back. Leave sts on a spare needle.

Left front

Same as right front, reversing shapings.

Sleeves

Using No.2 needles and main color, cast on 57 sts and work in single ribbing for 2¾in. Next RS row: knit, inc into every 5th st (66 sts). Change to No.4 needles and work a bobble grid as for the back, positioning thus: row 1: p17, MB, p31, MB, p17.
Keep working the grid, as set, working a horizontal row as for the body but on the 9th and every following 48th row. Meanwhile inc 1 st each end of every 25th/15th row, keeping all new sts in the pattern as you go, but omitting any bobbles that fall right at the edge of the work. When there are 77/85 sts the sleeve should measure 17/18in. If short, work a few rows straight to achieve the correct length.
Shape sleeve cap: bind off 5 sts at beg of next 2 rows. Now dec 1 st each end of every row until 61/63 sts remain. Dec 1 st each end of every other row until 31 sts remain. Bind off 4 sts at beg of next 4 rows. Bind off remaining sts.

Front bands

Using No.2 needles and main color, cast on 10 sts and work in single ribbing until the band is long enough to fit from the bottom of the waistband to the front edge of the neck when very slightly stretched. Leave the sts on a pin. Place a pin to mark the first button position, 5 rows from the cast-on edge. Divide the band equally and mark 6 more button positions, making allowance for the 8th being worked on

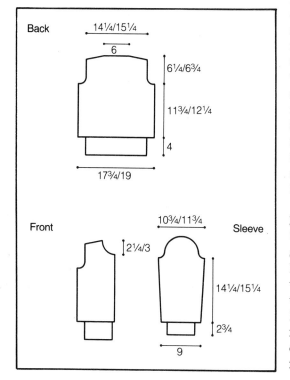

Back
14¼/15¼
6
6¼/6¾
11¾/12¼
4
17¾/19

Front
2¼/3

10¾/11¾
Sleeve
14¼/15¼
2¾
9

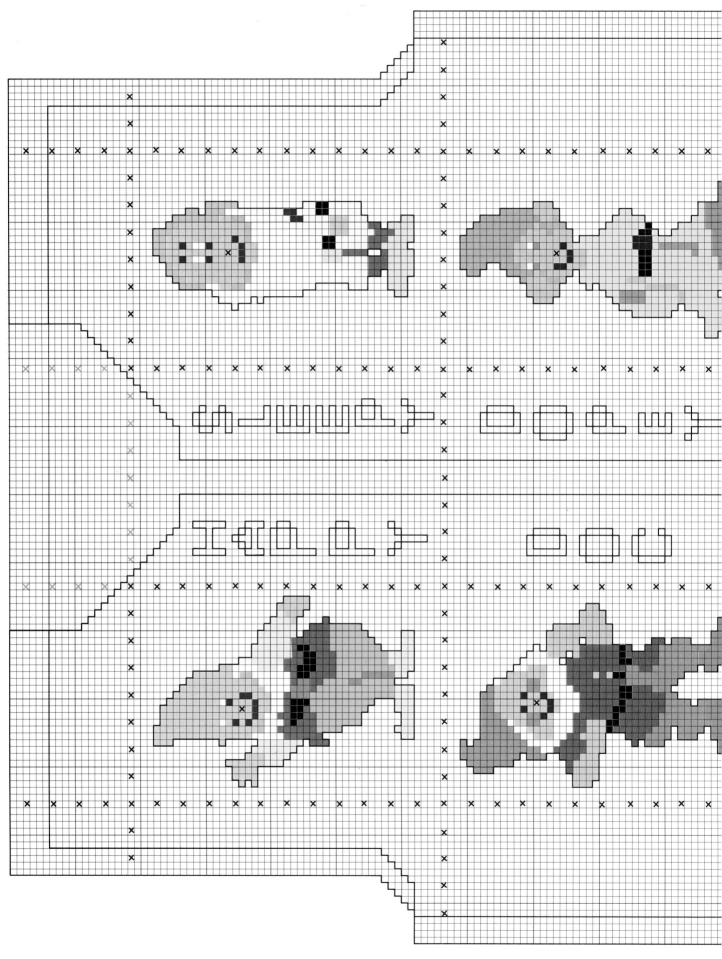

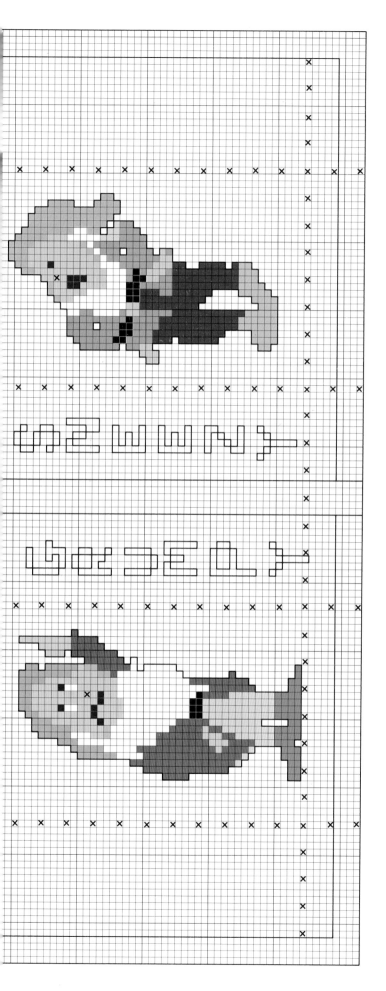
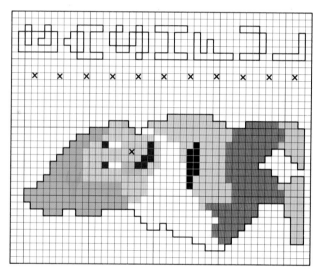

the neckband. Now work the buttonhole band to match, working buttonhole rows to correspond to marker pins thus: rib 4, bind off 2, rib 4. On the next row cast on 2 sts above those that were bound off, and then cont normally to next buttonhole row. When second band matches the first, leave sts on a pin.

Neckband

Knit both shoulder seams tog (*see* Techniques, pages 13-14), and leave the 45 back neck sts on a spare needle.

Using No.2 needles and main color, rib the right-front sts onto the needle and with the RS of work facing, knit up 20/26 sts along right side of neck, knit the back neck sts on to the same needle and then knit up 20/26 sts down the left side of the neck, finishing by ribbing the left band sts (105/117 sts). Work in single ribbing for 3 rows. Work a buttonhole to correspond with the others. Rib 2 more rows and bind off in ribbing.

Shoulder pads

Using No.4 needles and 2 strands of main color yarn, cast on 2 sts. Cont in garter st (knit every row), inc 1 st each end of every row until you have 26 sts. Now work straight for 1½in. Bind off. Work 2 the same.

Finishing

Carefully pin the bands to the fronts, making sure that they are even. Attach with a flat seam. Join the side and sleeve seams with a flat seam over the ribbing and a narrow backstitch over the pattern. Set the sleeves in last, distributing the sleeve head evenly around the armhole. Pin and backstitch.

Attach the buttons where the marker pins indicate and tack the shoulder pads inside the cardigan as described on pages 15-16.

TWEEDLEDUM AND TWEEDLEDEE WOMEN'S CARDIGAN

A V-neck "boxing" cardigan for men and women – the terrible twins battling it out on the front while the back is emblazoned with their names, in the prize-fighting tradition. Worked in worsted weight wool, instructions are one-size women's/one-size men's, the raglan sleeves making it an easy-to-wear shape for anyone.

Back

Using No.4 needles and main color, cast on 128/140 sts.

Row 1: *k1, p1, rep from * to end. This row forms single ribbing; work in exactly the same way wherever ribbing is required within the instructions.

Rib for 1¾in, change to red and rib ¾in, return to main color and rib ¾in. Change to No.6 needles and cont in st st until the work measures 11½/12¼in, ending with a WS row. Next row: k24/30, k the first row from the lettering chart, k to end. Cont working chart as set until work measures 14¼/15in, ending with a WS row.

Shape raglan (cont to work chart throughout): bind off 2 sts at beg of next 2 rows. Next row: k2, sl 1, k1, psso, k to last 4 sts, k2 tog, k2. Row 2: purl. Repeat these two rows until the chart is complete. Now cont in main color, shaping raglan as before until 36/42 sts remain. Work 3/4 rows straight. Bind off.

Right front

Using No.4 needles and main color, cast on 62/68 sts and work in striped single ribbing, as for back, until work measures 2¼in, ending with a WS row. Change to No.6 needles and work in st st for 4 rows.

Next row: k3/6, k the first row of the Tweedledum chart, k to end. Work chart in this position until it is complete. Meanwhile, when work measures 14¼/15in, **shape raglan**: next WS row bind off 2 sts, work to end. Row 2: k to last 4 sts, k2 tog, k2. Row 3: purl. Repeat these 2 rows until 52/58 sts remain.

Shape neck: dec 1 st at neck edge on next and every following 4th row, meanwhile cont to shape raglan as before. When 12/9 sts remain work the neck edge straight and cont to shape raglan until 4 sts remain.

Next row: purl. Row 2: k2, k2 tog. Row 3: purl. Row 4: k1, k2 tog. Work 2 rows straight. Bind off.

Left front

Same as right front until the chart and then: k5/8, k first row of the Tweedledee chart, k to end. Now cont as for right front, reversing the shapings and working the raglan decs as sl 1, k1, psso.

Sleeves

Using No.4 needles, on 52/58 sts and work in striped single ribbing, as for back, for 2¼in. Change to No.6 needles and cont in st st, inc 1 st each end of next and every following 5th row, until there are 100/110 sts. Now work straight until the sleeve measures 16¾/19½in from the beg, ending with a WS row. **Shape raglan**: bind off 2 sts at beg of next 2 rows. Now dec 1 st each end of next and every following knit row, as on the back, until there are 12 sts left. Bind off.

Buttonband

Using No.4 needles and main color, bind on 8 sts and work in single ribbing until the band is long enough to reach to the middle of the back neck when very slightly stretched. Leave on a pin. Divide the band into 4 sections from the very bottom to the point where the front neck shaping starts. Using safety pins, mark the

Materials

Yarnworks worsted weight wool – black: 20/22oz; red: 3½oz; contrast colors: less than 1oz of each of the 9 colors, matched exactly to the charts.
Both sizes require 5 buttons.

Needles

One pair of No.4 and one pair of No.6 needles.

Gauge

Using No.6 needles and measured over st st: 24 sts and 32 rows = 4in square.
NOTE: To avoid puckering, keep your gauge the same when working the color motifs. Do not carry the main color behind the motifs.

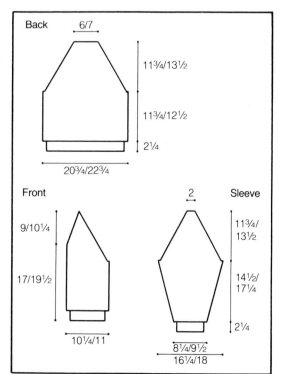

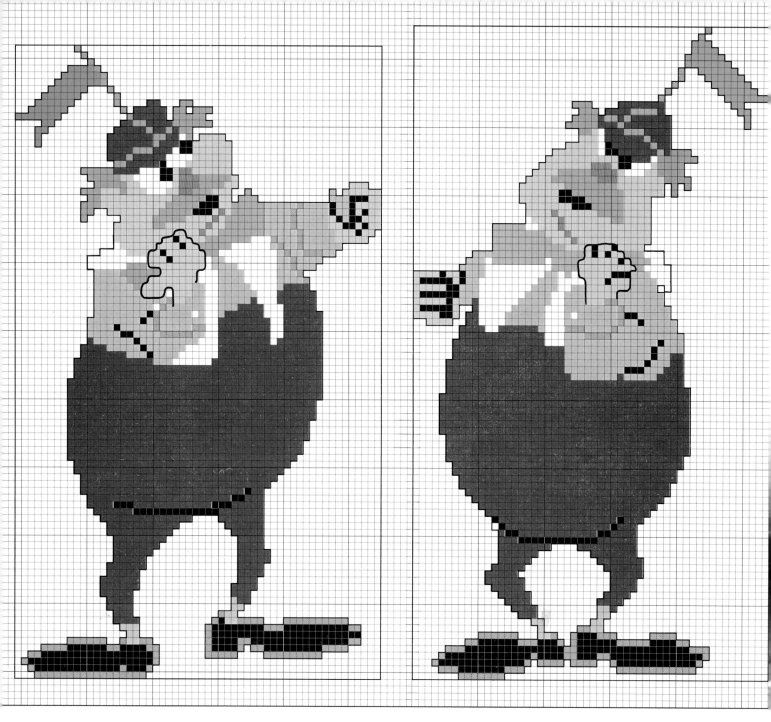

Tweedledum   **Tweedledee**

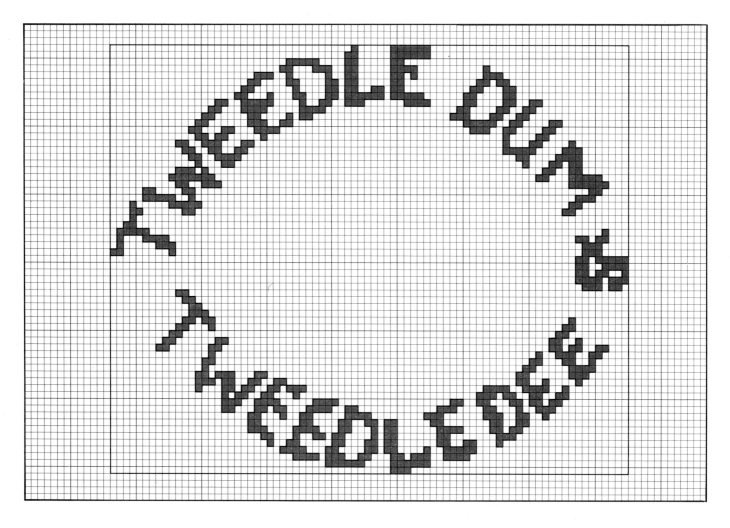

button positions, spacing them equally between the top and bottom positions.

Buttonhole band
Work as for the buttonband but working buttonhole rows where the marker pins indicate, thus: buttonhole row: rib 3, bind off 2, rib 3. Next row: rib, casting on 2 sts immediately above those bound off on the previous row.
Work the band until it is the same length as the other. Leave sts on a pin.

Finishing
Throughout the seams are flat. Join the raglans first, followed by the sleeve and side seams. Now knit the two ends of the front bands tog, place this seam at the center back neck of the cardigan and pin the bands to the fronts, taking care to distribute them evenly. Join with a very careful flat seam. Attach buttons where marker pins indicate.
Using backstitch, embroider the outline of the twin's fists in black yarn.

WINNIE THE POOH LAYETTE

An Eeyore dress, a Piglet cardigan and shorts outfit and a Pooh romper suit – all quoted in sizes for 6/9/12/18 month-old babies (see diagrams for sizing). All garments are worked in royal blue sport weight wool, with contrast colors matched exactly to the charts.

EEYORE DRESS

Back

Using No.3 needles and main color, cast on 124/132/140/148 sts.
Row 1: *k1, p1, rep from * to end. Repeat this row to form single ribbing. Rib for 6 rows and then change to No.4 needles and cont in st st until work measures 9¾/10¾/11½/12¼in.
Next RS row: knit, working a dec every 3rd st (83/88/94/99 sts). Change to No.3 needles and work in k1, p1 ribbing for 2/2¼/2¾/3¼in.
Shape armholes: bind off 6/6/7/7 sts at beg of

Materials
Yarnworks sport weight wool – **dress**: 6/6/8/8oz; **cardigan** 6/6/6/6oz; **shorts**: 3½/3½/3½/3½oz; **romper suit**: 8/8/8/9oz; contrast colors: less than 1oz of all contrast colors, matched exactly to the charts.
The dress requires a few inches of thin pink ribbon and 12in of black yarn for Eeyore's tail and bow; 2 snap fasteners and small metal buttons to stitch over them.
The shorts require elastic, ¾in wide, length to suit.
The cardigan requires 4 snap fasteners and small metal buttons to be tacked over them.
The romper suit requires 5 snap fasteners and small metal buttons to stitch over them.

Needles
One pair of No.2, one pair of No.3 and one pair of No.4 needles.

Gauge
Using No.4 needles and measured over st st: 28 sts and 36 rows = 4in square.
NOTE: To avoid puckering, keep your gauge the same when working the color motifs. Do not carry the main color behind the motifs.

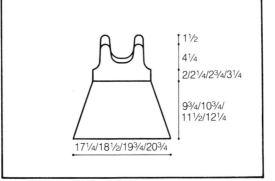

1½
4¼
2/2¼/2¾/3¼
9¾/10¾/11½/12¼
17¼/18½/19¾/20¾

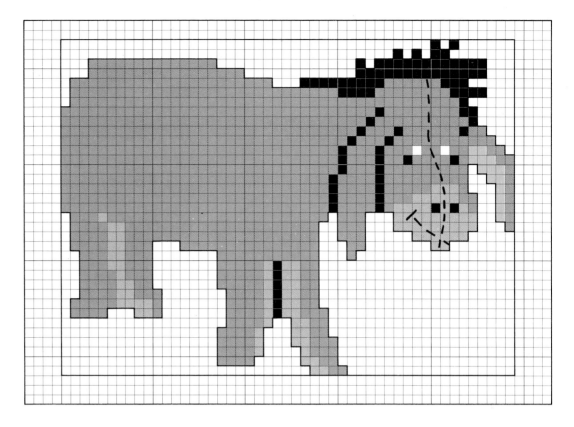

next 2 rows. Now dec 1 st each end of every row, 2 sts in from the edge and keeping in ribbing throughout until 63/68/72/77 sts remain. Work straight until work measures 4¾in from beg of bodice ribbing.

Shape neck: rib 23/24/25/26 sts, bind off 17/20/22/25 sts, rib to end. Cont with this set of sts, leaving others on a holder. Dec 1 st at neck edge, 2 sts in from edge, on every row until 18 sts remain. Cont straight, in ribbing, until the work measures 7/7½/7¾/8¼in from beg of bodice ribbing. Now dec 1 st each end of every row, 1 st in from edge, until 4 sts remain. Bind off as usual (i.e., not in ribbing). Return to other side of neck and work to match the first side.

Front

Same as back until work measures 2¼in, ending with a WS row.

Next row: k66/72/78/84, knit from Eeyore chart, joining in colors as required. Knit to end. Cont to work chart in this position until it is complete. Now work as for back until the ribbed bodice measures 3½/3½/4¼/4¼in. **Shape neck**: as for back but working each strap to a length of 5½/6/6¼/6¾in from beg of bodice ribbing before shaping the end.

Finishing

Join sides with a flat seam. Attach snap fasteners to straps according to size, and stitch one button on top of each fastener. Cut three 4in lengths of black yarn and knot them together at one end, plaiting the strands to form Eeyore's tail. Secure the end by tying a small length of pink ribbon into a bow and stitch through this bow with matching thread to prevent it from coming undone. Attach the tail to Eeyore's rear. Embroider the facial features, as illustrated, using backstitch.

PIGLET CARDIGAN

Back

Using No.3 needles and main color, cast on 76/80/84/88 sts.
Row 1: *k2, p2, rep from * to end. Repeat this row to form double ribbing for 1in. Change to No.4 needles and cont in st st until work measures 10¾/11/11½/11¾in. Leave sts on a spare needle.

Left front

Using No.3 needles and main color, cast on 36/40/40/44 sts and work in double ribbing for 1in. Change to No.4 needles and cont in st st until the work measures 8¾/9/9½/9¾in, ending with a RS row. **Shape neck**: bind off 4 sts at the beg of the next row. Now dec 1 st at neck edge on every row until 21/23/24/26 sts remain. Leave sts on a spare needle.

Right front

Same as left front until work measures 3¼in, ending with a WS row. Next row: k5/7/7/9 sts, k the first row from the Piglet chart, k to end. Cont working the chart in this position until it is completed. Now cont in main color st st until work measures 8¾/9/9½/9¾in, ending with a WS row. **Shape neck**: as for the left front. Leave sts on a spare needle.

Sleeves

Using No.2 needles and main color, cast on 40/40/44/44 sts and work in double ribbing for 2 rows. **Change to fuchsia, knit 1 row, rib 1 row. Return to main color, knit 1 row, rib 3 rows.** Rep from ** to **. Knit the next row, inc into every 5th/4th/5th/4th st (48/50/52/55 sts). Change to No.4 needles and cont in st st, inc 1 st each end of 3rd/6th/1st/3rd and every following 3rd/3rd/4th/4th row until you have 74/78/82/85 sts. Work straight until the sleeve measures 6/6¾/7½/8¼in. Bind off.

Neckband

Knit both shoulder seams tog (*see* Techniques pages 13-14), leaving the middle 34/34/36/36 back neck sts on a spare needle. Using a No.2 needle, main color and with RS facing, knit up 18/18/21/21 sts around the right side of neck, knit the back neck sts onto the same needle and then knit up 18/18/21/21 sts down the right side of the neck. Work in double ribbing for 1in. Bind off in ribbing.

Front bands

Using No.2 needles, main color and with RS of the right front facing, knit up 74/78/82/86 sts evenly from the very bottom edge to the top edge of the neckband. Work in double ribbing for 1in. Bind off in ribbing. Work the left front band to match.

Finishing

Lay work flat and pin sleeves into position, taking care not to bunch them. Sew with backstitch. Join the sleeve and side seams with a flat seam over the ribbing, backstitch over the st st. Attach the snap fasteners to the front bands and stitch a button on top of each. Embroider Piglet's facial features, as illustrated, using backstitch and satin stitch.

PIGLET SHORTS

Back

Start at the lower edge of the left leg. Using No.3

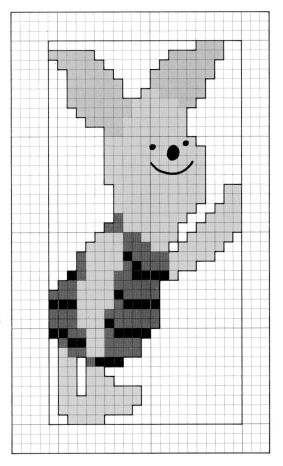

needles and main color, cast on 32/36/36/40 sts. Work in double ribbing for 2 rows. Now work from ** to ** as for the cardigan sleeves twice. Rib 2 more rows. Knit the next row, inc into every 3rd/4th/4th/5th st (42/45/45/48 sts). Now change to No.4 needles and cont in st st, until work measures 4/4½/4¾/5¼in, ending with a WS row. **Shape crotch**: next row bind off 3 sts,

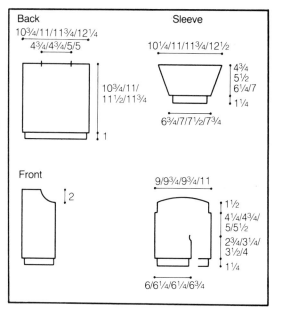

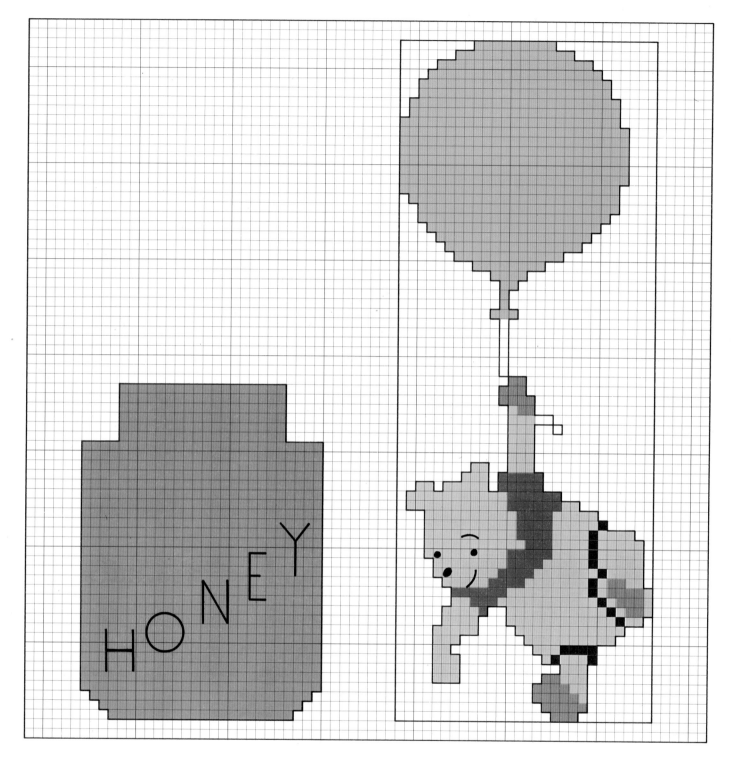

work to end. Dec 1 st at crotch edge on next 4 rows. Leave these sts on a spare needle. Work the right leg to match, reversing shapings. Now slip the left leg sts onto the same needle, crotch shapings to the middle of the row. Next row (WS): purl. Row 2: k32/35/35/38, k2 tog through back loops (tbl), k2, k2 tog, k to end. Purl one row and then knit the next row, dec 1 st either side of middle 2 sts as on row 2

(66/72/72/78 sts). Work straight until work measures 8¼/9¼/9¾/10¾in.

Shape waist: next row work to last 10 sts, turn and repeat. 3rd and 4th rows: work to last 20 sts, turn and repeat. 5th and 6th rows: work to last 30 sts, turn and repeat. Break off yarn and slip all sts onto the same needle. Now work across all sts, dec 1 st in every 10 sts. Cont in st st for a further 16 rows. Bind off.

Front

Work right leg as for back left leg until work measures 4/4½/4¾/5¼in, ending with a RS row. **Shape crotch**: dec 1 st at crotch edge on next 4 rows. Leave these sts on a spare needle and work a left leg to match. Now work as for back, but dec 1 st each side of central 2 sts on 4 RS rows in all (64/70/70/76 sts). Cont as for back but omitting the turned rows.

Finishing

Join seams with a flat seam, leaving the waist seam open for ¾in at the very top on one side. Turn in the bound off edge and slip st it down inside the waist to form a tube ¾in deep. Thread elastic through the opening that has been left and join the ends according to waist size.

POOH ROMPER SUIT

Back

Start at the lower edge of the left leg. Using No.2 needles and blue, cast on 32/33/35/36 sts and work in single ribbing for 5 rows. *Change to red and purl the next row. Work the following row in ribbing, as previously set. Change back to blue and purl the next row. Work 4 more rows in ribbing as previously set.* Rep from * to * once more. Work 5 more rows in ribbing and then change to st st, inc into every 3rd st (42/44/46/48 sts). Change to No.4 needles and cont in st st until work measures 6¾/7/7½/7¾in, ending with a WS row.

Shape crotch: next row bind off 3 sts, work to end. Row 2: purl. Row 3: **k1, k2 tog, k to end.** Rep last 2 rows (37/39/41/43 sts). Leave these sts on a spare needle.

Work the right leg to match, reversing shapings and dec by k2 tog through back loops (tbl). Now slip the left leg sts onto the same needle, crotch shapings to the middle of the row. Next row (WS): purl. Row 2: k34, k2 tog tbl, k2, k2 tog, k to end (72/76/80/84 sts). Work straight until work measures 12½/13½/14½/15in. Change to No.2 needles and cont in single ribbing for 1¼in. Return to No.4 needles and cont in st st until work measures 14¾/15¾/16¾/17¼in.

Form sleeves: cast on 33/36/39/42 sts at beg of next 2 rows. Now work straight until work measures 19/20/21/21½in. Next RS row **shape neck**: k54/58/62/66 sts, bind off 30/32/34/36 sts, k to end. Cont with this set of sts, leaving others on a holder. Dec 1 st at neck edge on next 2 rows. Work 2 rows straight. Leave sts on a holder. Return to the other side of neck and shape to match. Leave sts on a holder.

Left front

Work from bottom of left leg as for back of right leg until work measures 6¾/7/7½/7¾in ending with a RS row. Shape crotch: next row bind off 4 sts, work to end. Row 2: k to last 3 sts, k2 tog tbl, k1. Row 3: purl. Rep these last 2 rows another 2 times more (35/37/39/41 sts).

Cont as for back until work measures 14¾/15¾/16¾/17¼in. **Form sleeve**: next RS row cast on

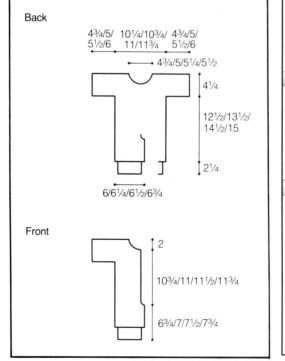

Back

4¾/5/ 5½/6   10¼/10¾/ 11/11¾   4¾/5/ 5½/6

4¾/5/5¼/5½

4¼

12½/13½/ 14½/15

2¼

6/6¼/6½/6¾

Front

2

10¾/11/11½/11¾

6¾/7/7½/7¾

33/36/39/42 sts, work to end. Cont straight until work measures 17½/18/19/19½in , ending with a RS row. **Shape neck**: bind off 8 sts and work to end. Dec 1 st at neck edge on every row until 52/56/60/64 sts remain. Now work straight until the front matches the back. Leave sts on a holder.

Right front

This is worked as for left front, reversing shapings, but when work measures 3½in, ending with a WS row, incorporate the Winnie the Pooh chart. Next row: k8/9/10/11, work chart sts, joining in colors where necessary, k to end. Work chart in this position until it is complete and then cont as for left side.

Pocket

Using No.4 needles and tan yarn, cast on 20 sts. Work in st st, inc 1 st each end of every row for 3 rows. Now work straight until it measures 3¼in. Next RS row: *k2 tog, k2, rep from * to end. Change to No.2 needles and work in single ribbing for 6 rows. Bind off normally (i.e., not in ribbing).

Front bands

Make 2

Using No.2 needles and main color, with RS facing, knit up 82/86/90/94 sts along the straight edge of the front and work in single ribbing for 10 rows. Bind off normally (i.e., not in ribbing) but taking care to keep the gauge correct so that this edge will not pull in.

Neckband

Knit one shoulder seam tog, bind off the 34/36/38/40 sts for the back neck and then knit the other shoulder seam tog (*see* Techniques, pages 13-14). Using No.2 needles and with RS of work facing, knit up 90/94/98/102 sts around the neckline from the outer edge of the right front band to the outer edge of the left front band. Purl the first row and then work 3 rows in single ribbing. Now work as for leg ribbing (page 90) from * to *. Bind off in ribbing.

Right cuff

Using No.2 needles, blue yarn and with RS facing, knit up 48/50/52/54 sts from back edge to front edge of cuff. Purl the first row and then work 3 rows in single ribbing. Now work as for leg ribbing from * to * twice. Bind off in ribbing. Work left cuff the same, but knit up sts from front to back edge.

Finishing

Join sleeve side and leg seams with a flat seam on ribbing, a narrow backstitch over the st st. Overlap the base edges of the front bands and sew with slip stitch to the bound off edge at the crotch. Embroider the word "honey" on the pocket, as illustrated, using backstitch. Lightly press the pocket and then position on the breast, above the ribbing and carefully sew with slipstitch around the edge.
Embroider Pooh's facial features, as illustrated, using backstitch and satin stitch.
Attach the snap fasteners, placing one at the neckband, one 2in up from the base of the bands and spacing the others equally between. Stitch a button on top of each.

ABBREVIATIONS

beg	begin(ning)
cont	continue/continuing
dec	decrease/decreasing
in	inch(es)
inc	increase/increasing
k	knit
LH	left hand
MB	make bobble (*see* Techniques, page 11).
m 1	make one – i.e., inc 1 st by working from the stockinette below the next st to be worked
p	purl
psso	pass slipped stitch over
rep	repeat
rev st st	reverse stockinette st
RH	right hand
RS	right side
sl	slip
st(s)	stitch(es)
st st	stockinette stitch
tbl	through back of loop(s)
tog	together
WS	wrong side

YARN INFORMATION

All the sample garments illustrated in this book
were knitted in Yarnworks yarns. As many of the
designs contain small quantities of several
different colors, Yarnworks offers individual kits
containing only the quantities of yarn necessary
to complete each garment. Each kit contains
enough yarn to knit up to the largest size
indicated on the pattern; in addition, buttons,
embroidery threads and trimmings are included
where appropriate. Although authentic Disney
approved colors must be used for the motifs,
some designs may be knitted in a choice of
background colors.

   To order, simply contact Marcus Corps, 117
Dobbins Street, Brooklyn 11222, New York, or
telephone 718 383 7321.

   For those who wish to substitute different
yarns, weights are given throughout to the
nearest 2oz ball. To obtain the best results you
must ensure that the gauge recommended on
your selected yarn *matches the gauge* printed in
our pattern. We cannot guarantee your results if
this rule is not followed.